MIDDLE MANAGERS IN EUROPE

What role is there for middle managers in Europe today?

Based on research from the European Human Capital and Mobility Programme and focusing specifically on the role of middle managers and the management of change within different types of companies, this book provides an overview of the evolution of middle management in Europe and includes:

- a comparative analysis using empirical evidence to show how their role has changed
- an analysis of the evolution of managerial practices and the attitudes of middle managers to them in the UK, France, Denmark and Greece
- an exploratory study of the consequences of quality management on middle managers.

This research contains the findings and views from members of fifteen organizations from five European countries – Greece, France, Portugal, The Netherlands and the UK.

Yves-Frédéric Livian is Professor at the IAE, University Jean Moulin and associate researcher at the IRE, Management Research Institute, Lyon. **John G. Burgoyne** is Professor of Management Learning at The Management School, Lancaster University.

ROUTLEDGE ADVANCES IN MANAGEMENT AND BUSINESS STUDIES

MIDDLE MANAGERS
IN EUROPE

*Edited by Yves-Frédéric Livian
and John G. Burgoyne*

London and New York

First published 1997
by Routledge
11 New Fetter Lane, London EC4P 4EE

Simultaneously published in the USA and Canada
by Routledge
29 West 35th Street, New York, NY 10001

©1997 Yves-Frédéric Livian and John G. Burgoyne

Typeset in Palatino by Florencetype Ltd, Stoodleigh, Devon

Printed and bound in Great Britain by TJ Press (Padstow) Ltd,
Padstow, Cornwall

British Library Cataloguing in Publication Data
A catalogue record for this book is available from the British Library

Library of Congress Cataloguing in Publication Data
A catalogue record for this book has been requested

ISBN 0–415–13902–3

CONTENTS

CONTENTS

FIGURES

TABLES

NOTES ON CONTRIBUTORS

Prof. Frank Bournois, Professor at IAE-University Jean Moulin Lyon 3, 15 quai Claude Bernard, 69007 Lyon, France.

Prof. John G. Burgoyne, Department of Management Learning, The Management School, University of Lancaster, Lancaster, LA14YX, United Kingdom

Dr Sue Dopson, University Lecturer in Management Studies (Organizational Behaviour), Templeton College, Oxford OX1 5NY, United Kingdom.

Dr Stella Kufidu, Associate Professor, Department of Business Administration, University of Macedonia, 156 Egnatia, 54006 Thessaloniki, Greece.

Dr Henrik Holt Larsen, Associate Professor, Copenhagen Business School, Institute of Organization and Industrial Sociology, Blaagaardsgade 23B, DK-2200 Copenhagen n, Denmark.

Prof. Yves-Frédéric Livian, Associate Researcher at IRE, Groupe ESC Lyon, 23 av Guy de Collongue, BP 174, 69132 Ecully Cedex, France: Professor at IAE, University Jean Moulin Lyon 3, 15 quai Claude Bernard, 69007 Lyon, France.

Dr Dimitrios M. Mihail, Lecturer, Department of Business Administration, University of Macedonia, 156 Egnatia, 54006 Thessaloniki, Greece.

Dr Jean Neumann, Co-ordinator, Programme for Organizational Change and Technological Innovation, Tavistock Institute, 30 Tabernacle Street, London, EC2A 4DD, United Kingdom.

Dr Helen Newell, Lecturer in Industrial Relations, Warwick University, Warwick, United Kingdom.

Dr Eugenia Petridu, Lecturer, Department of Economics, Aristotle University, Thessaloniki, Greece.

Michel Rousselot, President of 'Eurocadres', Council of European Professional and Managerial Staff, Bruxelles, Belgium; Eurocadres, 47 avenue S. Bolivar, 75950 Paris Cedex 19, France.

Dr Jean-Pierre Segal, Research Fellow, 'Gestion et Société' Centre, Equipe de recherche du CNRS, 140 rue du Chevaleret, 75013 Paris, France; Professor at Ecole des Ponts et Chaussées (France).

Dr Philippe Trouvé, Professor at ESC Clermont-Ferrand, 4 Bd Trudaine, 63037 Clermont-Ferrand, France; director of CER (associate research centre to Cereq) Centre d'Etudes et de Recherches sur les Qualifications (France).

Prof Maarten Rudolf Van Gils, Faculty of Management and Organization, University of Groningen, PO Box 800, 9700 Av Groningen, Netherlands.

Fotis Vouzas, Assistant, Department of Business Administration, University of Macedonia, 156 Egnatia, 54006 Thessaloniki, Greece.

FOREWORD

This book is a result of a research programme carried out from 1992 to 1995 under the 'Management effectiveness' theme of the 'European competitiveness in a knowledge society' project in the Human Capital and Mobility Programme, DG XII, Brussels. The purpose of that programme was to create a European research network[1] able to support the training and development of young researchers and to develop exchanges in topics considered to be of critical importance for the European Union.

Two themes have been distinguished but are strongly connected:

- Middle managers, which is the theme of this book
- Knowledge workers, which is the theme of another book also published by Routledge.[2]

The two research teams organized a joint conference, 'Knowledge work, managerial roles and European competitiveness' held in ESC Lyon from 30 November to 3 December 1994, where other academics have been invited to give papers. This conference also invited executives from different countries. The present book is mainly built on the papers related to the 'Middle managers' topic presented at that conference.

Prof. Yves F. Livian
Prof. John G. Burgoyne

NOTES

1 The institutions members are University of Lancaster (UK), University of Porto (Portugal), University of Thessaloniki (Greece),

University of Groningen (Netherlands), Copenhagen Business School (Denmark) and Groupe ESC Lyon (France).

2 *Knowledge Work, Organization and Expertise: A European Perspective*, F. Blackler, D. Courpasson and B. Elkjaer, (eds) London: Routledge, 1997 (forthcoming).

ACKNOWLEDGEMENTS

We are indebted to the DG XII of the European Commission for financing the field study in five countries and the Lyon Conference (Human Capital and Mobility Programme, no. CHRX CT93-0232).

This project would not have been possible without the competence and energy of the University of Lancaster Management School staff, and especially Professor A. Mercer and Sue Hird. Thanks to Catherine Cesari for preparing the typescript.

ABBREVIATIONS

APL   accreditation of prior learning
CEO   chief executive officer
DPO   Danish Patent Office
EU   European Union
HR   human resources
HRM   human resource management
ILO   International Labour Organization
INSEE   Institut National de la Statistique et des Etudes
        Economiques
IPM   Institute of Personnel Management
ISO   International Organization for Standards
IT   information technology
JIT   just in time
MM   middle manager
OD   organizational development
P&MS   professional and managerial staff
QC   quality circles
R&D   research and development
TQM   total quality management

1

INTRODUCTION

Middle managers in management thinking: crucial ... and absent

Yves-Frédéric Livian

The place of middle managers (MMs) in management thinking has always been ambivalent: on one hand, MMs are viewed as critical actors of corporate performance and change. On the other hand, they are almost absent as objects of analysis and prescriptions.

To give just a few examples, strategic management literature considers the MM as crucial providers of information to upper levels. In his critique of strategic planning, Mintzberg (1994) notes that MMs get direct qualitative information which is priceless for strategic decision-making. They also hold 'tacit knowledge' which is essential for strategy formation. Nonaka (1988) considers that the only managerial style adapted to the intensity of market competition and speed required for efficient information creation is a 'middle-up down' management. The core of this style is MMs, well equipped with ability to combine macro and hands-on information.

Total quality management (TQM) literature insists on the crucial role of MMs as change agents, in order to implement the new practices and the new philosophy carried by TQM. Of course another popular topic, 'empowerment', underlines the necessity of more flexibility and innovation to decentralize responsibilities to the lower levels and could threaten MMs pivotal role. But many authors and executives immediatly reply that this is not the case, and that empowerment does not mean a decreasing role of MMs (Eccles, 1994).

But who are the actors on the stage of traditional management thinking? First, there is a vague group, the 'human resources' (HR), in which intermediate categories of staff are included, but

1

often without any special notice. According to the business school-type literature, it is admitted that HR are a crucial asset, and that company development must rely on effective HR development. But there are only very few references to the specific situation of MMs. The larger part of management literature deals with the people taking the most important decisions, at the upper level of hierarchies – executives (or 'top managers') in general, or more specific types of functions, such as chief executive officers (CEOs) or general managers (for example, Kotter, 1982, Kurke and Aldrich, 1983).

Since management techniques are supposedly used by decision-makers, it is rational to study their roles and to provide them with techniques and tools helping them to rule the organization. In a way (such it has been advanced very cleverly) management has been more in line with the Fayol's heritage than with Taylor's.

Generations of managers have been trained with case studies where they are expected to analyse facts and take decisions as if they were executives. Sometimes, it is difficult to make clear that most of the management students will not, unfortunately for them, become executives. Sometimes the term 'manager' appears, designating a figure of management literature and research. Does this mean that, at last, we will give up the 'upper levels', and that we will go through the mass of intermediate managers ruling the day-to-day operations? Not so often, because studies or pieces of research dealing with 'managers' are in fact based on people at a high level of command. We can exemplify that by the seminal Mintzberg (1973) work for studying the roles of managers, but relying, as an empirical basis, on the observation of five chief executive officers (CEO).

A number of replications of Mintzberg observation have studied more modest levels in a wide variety of organizations, including schools and public agencies, and sometimes the results have been consistent with Mintzberg's views. But the starting-point was a study about CEOs. Fortunately, there has been an attempt to give a view of the 'life in the middle' (Kanter and Stein, 1979). Also, during the 1960s there have been specific studies on 'middle' managers (for example, Horne and Lupton, 1965, Sayles, 1964). Some classical studies about managers took into account the level of responsibilty (Stewart, 1967, 1982) but these have been very few. An international survey about the

2

evolution of managerial employment has taken place in the 1980s (Roomkin, 1991).

However, very often, when an analysis is made about managers, the rhetoric produced shows them as, for example, 'pathfinders' (Leavitt, 1986) 'sense makers', 'visionary', 'charismatic' etc, which does not consider those that are at the bottom of managerial lines! Many studies (perhaps the majority) about managerial work do not even make any distinction between managers and executives, assuming that management is a type of activity which is ready to be studied in itself, irrespective of the level of responsibilty of the managers studied. What is studied, for example, is 'leader behaviour' with universal tools (see, for example, LOS (Leadership Observation Survey) proposed by Luthans and Lockwood, 1984). Again, an interesting comparison about 'Euromanager' deals only with top managers (Eberwein and Tholen, 1993).

Focused on managerial activities, in general the bulk of research and literature has not considered sufficiently the different types of jobs and occupations in which these activities can be observed. One of the reasons why research on managerial activities (or leadership) is often deceptive is that it doesn't relate enough to organizational and social structures. If this is rectified, then a distinction between different types and levels of managerial occupations can be achieved – especially useful if we want to make any kind of international comparison. And it is striking that MMs have not been the focus of researchers attention so far.

MIDDLE MANAGERS: A FIRST DEFINITION

It is generally accepted that MMs are the product of organizational differentiation to the extent that it developed out of the increasing complexity of the internal division of labour (Reed, 1989). To other writers size is also a factor which influences the creation of this new managerial category (Ishikawa, 1985; Torrington and Weightman, 1987). Large and medium-sized companies create new layers of management in order to handle the demands of bureaucratic organizations. In contrast to the 'large organization' view, Dopson and Stewart (1993) point out that evidence from the 1981 British official census figures concerning 'managers in central and local government, industry and commerce' who generally 'plan and supervise in non-agricultural enterprises employing 25 persons and over' are a significant population who may also be thought of as MMs.

MMs relate differently in different nations' official occupational categories, which themselves affect educational and career development practice. In France, which has one of the most advanced systematic categories, the bulk of managers in organizational managerial careers are 'cadres administratifs et commerciaux d'entreprise'.[1] However, there are other categories relating to the broad definition: 'ingénieurs et cadres techniques d'entreprise', 'professions intermédiaires' and 'maîtrise d'entreprise' (which comprise foremen and forewomen/supervisors and first-line managers in these roles).

Several definitions of the MMs population can be identified. Kay identifies as MMs 'those who manage managers, supervisors or professional and technical people who are not Vice Presidents of functional or staff areas or General Managers, meaning that they have no profit or loss responsibilities' (Kay, 1974). Brennan defines them as 'general operational managers responsible for all operational decisions and the progress of the department, they have a number of supervisors below them and work closely with the department manager' (Brennan, 1991). Decision-making focus is the criterion that Breen (1984) uses and according to his definition MMs are 'people who are largely responsible for keeping the wheels of industry and commerce rolling. They do not necessarily make the big decisions, but they do make a multitude of smaller decisions, each of which could help or harm their organization'. Dopson et al. propose a broad definition of 'all those below the small group of top strategic managers and above first-level supervision' (Dopson et al. 1993). She gets very close to an old Kanter proposition according to which 'the middle is composed of a long stretch reaching from those with bare supervisory responsibility over lowest-level workers to those just below top policy-makers' (Kanter and Stein, 1979). Ishikawa (1985) simply distinguishes them as division heads and section chiefs.

Three closely related ideas appear to underpin these approaches to definition: middle of a command hierarchy; middle in terms of time-scale and scope of decision between strategic and routine supervision; middle in terms of organizational impact, between fundamental and inconsequential.

Given the supposed complexity and changing nature of modern organizations and the possibility of sector and national differences, a broad-ranging definition, following Dopson et al. (1993), of middle excluding the top and bottom of a hierarchy, and a broad interpretation of scope and impact, is probably most useful for working purposes.

Within that 'stretch', we can broadly distinguish two groups. First are those having responsibilities for the work of others, and having some kind of hierarchical power: they are often called 'field' or 'line' managers. 'Their middleness lies in being caught between those below, whose co-operation they need, and those above, who give them the authority to implement stated policy' (Kanter and Stein, 1979: 80).

Second, are the professionals, those having authority over their own work, subject to organizational rules and constraints, but exerting an influence on others mainly based on their technical competence. If we follow again Kanter, 'their middleness lies in their position between freedom and independence because of their expertise in their job, and the terms and conditions of their work, set by the formal authority and structure of the organization' (Kanter and Stein, 1979: 81)[2].

CHANGES IN MIDDLE MANAGEMENT: AN OVERVIEW OF THE LITERATURE

We have tried to analyse managerial literature about the changes which are supposed to affect middle managers.[3] The literature on MM change is characterized by assumptions, generalizations and future speculation. The bulk of the literature is a pessimistic outlook, from the point of view of the survival of MMs as a tradition, on the effect of the information technology (IT), new work and organization initiatives and structures on the numbers of, status of and opportunities for MMs. (Leavitt and Whistler, 1964; Neuman, 1978; Kanter, 1982; Drucker, 1988.)

Most consultants and organizational theory speculation supporting the 'pessimistic view' of MMs is opinion based, and involves the following predictions and assumptions:

- a demise of MMs due to IT
- a reduction in numbers of MMs due to IT, increased competition, cost reduction efforts and changing attitudes to authority

- a demand for radical change to avoid extinction – involving new roles, attitudes and skills for MMs.

Contrasting with these views are a smaller number of studies, some more evidence based, suggesting the opposite, that is of an enriching role for MMs. According to these studies MMs have greater responsibilities, more authority and more autonomy than before. The reduction in their numbers is not disproportional and is due to a slimming process applying to all managerial levels. Information technology has a positive effect, freeing MMs from the routine work and offering them an opportunity to be involved in the creative aspects of their jobs (Dopson et al., 1993; Pinsonneault and Kreamer, 1993). Some evidence also supports the proposition of increased involvement of MMs in strategy (Burgelman, 1983; Wooldridge and Floyd, 1990).

It is generally accepted that there are insufficient numbers of studies covering the MMs level (Torrington and Weightman, 1987). The existing studies have many drawbacks such as:

- building universal and sectoral generalizations
- small scale of studies
- studies tend to focus on so called excellent, exceptional or very large organizations and, therefore, possibly give a distorted picture
- few studies deal with national or sectoral differences
- absence of large-scale studies relating MM change to the realities of initiatives such as TQM, human resource management (HRM) and process re-engineering.

Within the literature fifteen propositions about the changing nature of MM can be identified: we present them grouped into seven broader topics.

Quantitative reduction

Reductions of the MM population is a much discussed topic. Zemke (1988) reported a 25 per cent reduction. Weiss (1988) locates downsizing as a phenomenon of the 1980s with MMs considered a 'useless overhead'. Dopson and Stewart (1993) suggest the interpretation of MMs reduction as part of a general slimming down of organizations. It is suggested that the introduction of just in time (JIT) systems transforms managerial hierarchies, reducing the need for MMs (Morgan, 1988).

Whether the reduction in MMs is time bound, sector related, following from any particular change in organizational arrangements or disproportionally large in relation to other organizational changes is not clear, though it is clear that, at least in the 1980s, it was greater than had been previously experienced (Fineman 1983; Nicholson and West 1988). One interpretation is that in some situations there is a finite period of MMs reduction, possibly following a similar period of operative worker reduction. During the early 1990s the American Management Association reported that MMs were only 5 per cent of the workforce and accounted for 22 per cent of the previous years layoffs (Dunaine, 1993). In Europe according to EUROSTAT 95, 'Managers and Professionals' have an average rate of unemployment of 9.4 per cent (from 2 per cent in Luxembourg to 17.7 per cent in Spain).

Reduced security and conventional career progression

Middle management is characterized by hard work, great pressure, less security and less promotion opportunities (Dopson, 1992). Inkson and Coe (1992) found that upward managerial moves are declining and MMs are increasingly subject to changes imposed by employers. Torrington and Weightman (1987) report that limitations on economic growth and organizational contradiction reduce the promotion prospects for MMs.

The downsizing trend during the 1980s, changes in production systems and IT and increases in employees' skill levels have brought about a decline in the need for MMs according to Weiss (1988), and in an increasing number of merger and acquisition situations MMs are vulnerable because they have 'old skills' in old jobs and tend to defend their positions rather that adapt to new conditions (Kay, 1974).

In France, several factors concur with a dramatic change of careers for intermediate and upper managers: development of fixed-term contracts, reduction of the corporate role in managing careers, increased demand for mobility and growth of redundancies for professionals and managers (Dany and Livian, 1995).

Changes to the content and the scope of their job

Reduction/change due to information technology

Information technology should cause MM to shrink (Leavitt and Whistler, 1964), disappear in its traditional role (Drucker 1970; Hicks 1971). These commentators suggest that IT has enabled senior managers to widen their span of control and reduce their dependence on MMs as links in a reporting chain and as passers of information. Dopson and Stewart (1993) found that IT poses a number of different challenges to MMs to improve their knowledge, skills and understanding of the nature of the organization's work.

Polakof (1987) argues that MMs do not have to fear the factory of the future. Production advances will not necessarily make MMs obsolete but will release MMs from routine co-ordination functions, freeing them to address issues of maximising efficiency and the full utilization of HR. Information technology can enrich MMs work by removing some of its more routine aspects (Dopson, 1992). Drucker (1970) and Gotlieb (1990) argue against the 'common supposition' that computers reduce the importance and the numbers of MMs, in favour of the view that the computer frees them for more important tasks and increase the demands on their abilities.

Incorporation of previously separate functions

In the simplification and delayering of organizations many specialist MMs functions are thought to have been removed with the work being done, if at all, by general MMs. This pattern is reported particularly in relation to the absorption of human resource management (personnel) into line management (Storey, 1992).

Less specific role and more role self-determination

Middle managers have become more generalist through assuming a wider range of responsibilties according to Storey (1992). Dopson (1992), Dopson et al. (1992) and Dopson and Stewart (1993) support this view in finding that the job of the MMs in emergent 'shallower' hierarchies has changed towards greater responsibilty with greater autonomy and a wider scope. Detailed, task-oriented job descriptions have become less important because of continuous change in jobs (Applegate et al., 1988).

Increased commitment to quality improvement and cost reduction

Increased commitment of MMs is portrayed as one of the pre-requisites of full TQM implementation, though there is little evidence to establish whether this hypothesized change is actu-ally occurring in MM. The rhetoric of TQM and HRM implies that increased commitment is the key to successful implemen-tation (Beer et al., 1984; Crosby, 1979; Ishikawa, 1985; Nonaka, 1988). The role of the MMs is high on the quality agenda. Middle managers are considered the key players in the implementation and maintenance of TQM initiatives (Nonaka, 1988; Collard, 1989; Hill, 1991; Wilkinson et al., 1993).

The opposite of commitment, that is, resistance or dissaffec-tion, occurs in the TQM literature. Most of the studies in TQM give evidence of a resistance of MMs populations to the intro-duction of quality circles, quality assurance systems and to the idea of quality generally. Foy (1981) suggests that MMs have tremendous capacity to block changes and Dopson et al. (1992) found that there is more resistance to changes in the public sector than in the private.

Middle managers are said to need to shift from a production manager orientation to a manufacturing manager/business manager orientation. In this mode, line managers seek to find ways of reducing costs, of improving quality and of deploying labour, materials and plant in new configurations which will add value to the process in hand. This 'business manager' has to be competent with SWOT analysis, planning, goal-setting, finance, marketing and the management of change, and to shift in orien-tation from technical to commercial aspects(Storey, 1992).

Less operational, more strategic and people-oriented roles

Less supervisory responsibility due to increased autonomy and self-direction of work groups

It is suggested that MMs jobs are changing to require a less con-trolling management style. The changing nature of organizations,

9

it is argued, has made close supervision obsolete. Managers should be more like coaches, counsellors and facilitators rather than decision-making controllers. Instead of trying to manage all the work group's activities, the manager should build self-management through teamwork (Kravetz, 1988). It is claimed that self-managed teams are taking over such standard supervision duties as scheduling work, maintaining quality, pay and vacations (Dunaine, 1993). In the self-managed team-based organization there are as many managers as before, but they are doing different things. They act less as supervisors and more as leaders, planners, strategists and project leaders (Carr, 1987; Kanter, 1986,). The flattening of organization structures requires new approaches to management and control. Managers have to co-ordinate the development of shared values and find the right balance between delegation and control – hands-off managing (Morgan, 1988). Ishikawa (1985) argues that MMs should strive to be people who do not always have to be physically present at the company, but to be indispensable to it.

Involvement in strategy.

Middle managers have arguably always played a key role in translating strategic change into operations (Smits, 1989). However, it is now argued that the MM role is becoming more strategic in itself, as opposed to being only operational (Dopson, 1992; Dopson and Stewart, 1993). It is suggested that MMs want to be included in strategy conversations for two reasons. They want access to powerful coalitions so that they can be influential in their work and carry out more meaningful roles for themselves. There is evidence of extensive dissatisfaction among MMs, who often perceive themselves as excluded from the strategic process (Westley, 1990).

Upward influence activity is reported as more prevalent in low risk/return types of strategic decisions than in high risk/return decisions, and also during the implementation rather than the formation of strategic decisions. Managers from private sector organizations exerted influence in both high risk and low risk strategic decisions more frequently than did managers from public sector organizations. Middle managers filter information and evaluate choices before the strategic decisions reach the top levels (Schilit, 1987). Burgelman (1983) points to the crucial role of MMs in supporting initiatives from operating levels, combining these with firm strengths, and conceptualizing them into new strategies. The contribution of MMs is claimed to be vital to strategy because they are often the first people to recognize strategic problems and opportunities (Nonaka, 1988; Wooldridge and Floyd, 1990).

Shift in balance of work from professional to managerial

In terms of the balance between technical, administrative and managerial work it is suggested that there is increased pressure on those who want career progress to move from the technical/ professional to the managerial (Torrington and Weightman, 1987). This shift from work termed 'professional/technical' to more 'management work' has been noted particularly in the public sector (Dopson et al., 1992).

Key players in moving from the 'old' to the 'new' style of HRM

Developments in British companies show that even without 'bidding' for a policy-making role in the HR area, MMs have been projected a more centre stage role in HRM. In addition to the requirements to be more 'up front' in directly briefing employees, the whole raft of measures involving managerial leadership, the shift towards individualized forms of pay, of more appraisal, of devolved management accountability, and of de-proceduralizing, all led to a more prominent role for MMs (Storey, 1992). In America, the business climate is reported as having shifted dramatically, and CEOs want staff to lead the change (Kanter, 1986). Middle managers must become the leaders of change (McDermont, 1992). The role of MMs is to work continually on improving the processes by involving the people, co-operating across functional boundaries and eliminating fear (Plowman, 1992).

New competencies for new roles

New set of roles

Teacher, coach, facilitator, entrepreneur, etc.: managers should be more like coaches, counsellors and facilitators than tight, decision-making controllers (Kravetz, 1988; Barry, 1992; McDermont, 1992; Wilkinson et al., 1993). The new entrepreneurial managers, called 'change masters', combine ideas with action (Kanter, 1986). A manager has to be teacher, counsellor, and friend as much as, or more than, commander, inspector and judge (Handy, 1991; Wisdom and Benton, 1992).

The entrepreneur, a figure of energy and drive, seizing opportunities to build up a successful business from scratch, is widely seen as a prime mover in the economy. The entrepreneurial set-up usually leaves managers with a great deal of autonomy. Despite the attraction of the term, there are severe difficulties in employing such as a general concept (Donaldson, 1985). Leaders or leadership is another approach suggested as a replacement for, or a new style in, management.

The new approach will come from politics, democracy, leadership, teams, co-ordination (Darwent, 1991). Turbulence and change will require organizations to adopt a much more pro-active and entrepreneurial relationship with their environment and to create new initiatives (Morgan, 1988). The new-style managers have to act as teachers instead of telling their employees what to do. Since organizations give to their employees more responsibilties, they will need to become more learning oriented (Wisdom and Benton, 1992).

'New contract' relationship: flexibility, creativity and innovation

The new-style manager, it is argued, has to work out how to improve performance. This is a creative act, an act of discovery rather than rule-following. Middle managers of the past were more likely to be preservers of territory than initiators of change. Innovate or perish is the slogan for the new management (Kanter, 1982). Beer et al. (1984) take a similar view in their approach to HRM arguing that the role of the manager is to be flexible and creative. Greater flexibility and adaptability as well as ability to learn new competencies is now a requirement for MMs (Dopson et al., 1992; Dopson and Stewart, 1993). Flexibility is the ability to anticipate and change rapidly in response to emerging business conditions (Kanter, 1986). The demands of an information society require organizations and their members to promote creativity, learning and innovation (Morgan, 1988). The prerequisites for the successful implementation of TQM is the ability of the managers to be flexible, able to release their creativity and contribute to quality improvement efforts (Deming, 1986, Juran, 1988).

Development of new attitudes and competencies

These changes require managers to exhibit participative rather than autocratic leadership, to build trust and influence others without direct challenge. For many these skills are new and have to be learnt (Storey, 1992). Managers must broaden their knowledge, learn new skills and become more adept in their capacity to influence others (McDermont, 1992; Stewart, 1991). Middle managers are said to need to develop new competencies and skills to cope with the changes. These include: strategic thinking; market awareness; client-centred thinking; better selection and management of human assets, material and financial skills (Dopson, 1992). History suggests that managerial competencies vary with the nature of environmental change; different events require different skills and abilities (Morgan, 1988).

Pressure and stress

The changing demands on MMs are in themselves felt and reported by many to increase pressure and stress. While there may be a tendency for all occupations at all times to report stress, there are grounds for believing that MMs is a special contemporary case. Value-added analysis, now used in many companies to determine each step in a work process, demands that MMs continually justify their existence and work (Kanter, 1986). The search for economy and efficiency puts the pressure on MMs to make effective, efficient and justifiable use of resources (Stewart, 1993a). With pressure and stress due to cutbacks, MMs are working longer hours and at weekends, and are treated less like management, more like part of the work-force (Levine, 1986; Zemke, 1988). The search for 'excellence' has an enormous psychological cost (Aubert and De Gaulejac, 1991). The trend towards 'lean, tough' organizations, automation of the workplace, the demand to adopt participative management styles while still meeting economic targets and dealing with changing social conditions among the managed are placing unusual pressures for MMs (Levine, 1986). In addition there is a reported

13

increasing inability to control workload, as opposed to work content, (Marshall and Cooper, 1977), in the context of constant pressure to update skills, knowledge and qualifications to retain status (Nicholson and West 1988). The imbalance between what is expected and the freedom to act is particularly stressful for MMs.

We have presented fifteen closely related forms of change believed to be affecting MMs and their work. The basis of these suggestions and claims varies enormously. A few are based on observation of small but general samples, or on general statistics, others are observations and extrapolations from single or small numbers of organizations which are likely to be atypical, though seen by commentators as exemplars of 'things to come'. Many claims are not explicit about their guarantors, that is, the basis within the claim or argument on which they might be believed (Mitroff and Bennis, 1993). Many claims are deductive in nature from a broad theoretical conceptualization of new, possibly normatively hoped for, forms of adaptative, flexible, 'learning' organizations (Burgoyne et al., 1994; Pedler et al., 1991). Other claims may appear to be based in rhetorical projects of 'talking up' a way of thinking about organizations and MMs to justify and legitimize some general or specific sets of organizational changes. In the most general sense, the change claims can be located along a scale from evidence-based to wish/opinion-based, as in Figure 1.1 taking account of kinds of arguments and 'guarantors' offered for the different claims.

This scale is interesting and possibly contentious not only from the point of view of its accuracy, but also from the point of view of the desirability of the different kinds of claim. By the conventional standards of representational research and science, evidence-based claims are to be privileged and preferred over rhetorical, wish-based and normative assertions. However, from a very different point of view of the role of social sciences, one where the central task is to create, invent and enact different social orders, then the rhetorical approach may be preferred provided that it is overt and explicit about this, rigorous in its own terms and concerned with the realizability of the construction of its visions. (See Chia (1994) for a treatment of this issue.) Equally, the wish or rhetoric-based claims for MMs can be interpreted as mythical, serving the function of giving MMs and

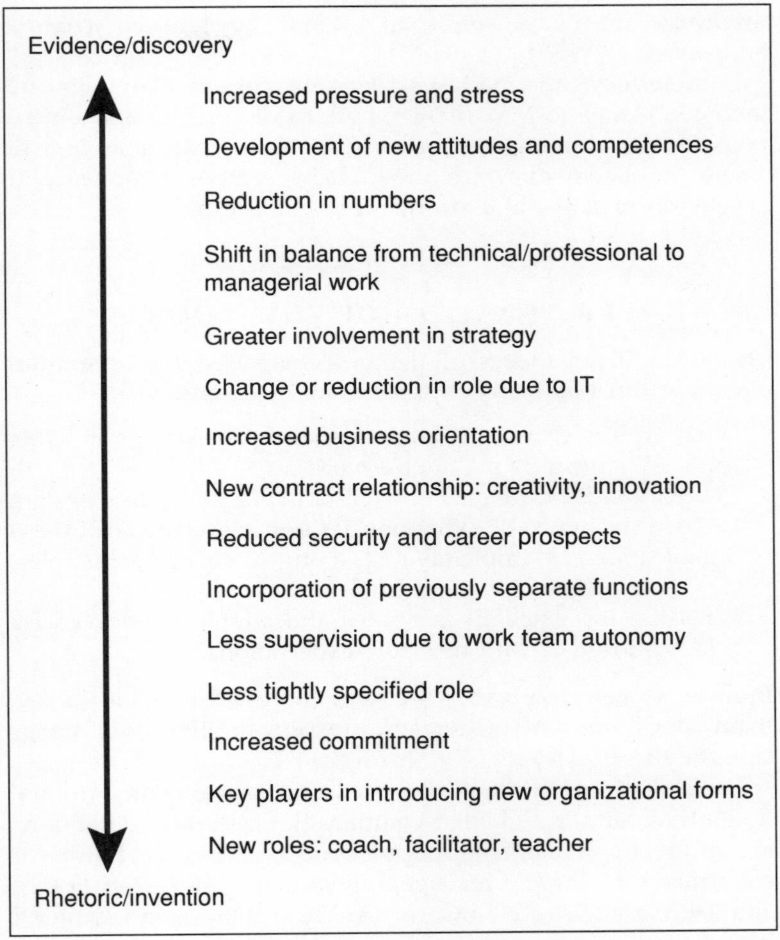

Evidence/discovery

↑

Increased pressure and stress

Development of new attitudes and competences

Reduction in numbers

Shift in balance from technical/professional to managerial work

Greater involvement in strategy

Change or reduction in role due to IT

Increased business orientation

New contract relationship: creativity, innovation

Reduced security and career prospects

Incorporation of previously separate functions

Less supervision due to work team autonomy

Less tightly specified role

Increased commitment

Key players in introducing new organizational forms

New roles: coach, facilitator, teacher

↓

Rhetoric/invention

Figure 1.1 MM change claims ordered on evidence/discovery – rhetoric/invention scale

others something to believe in, to make an otherwise harsh reality more tolerable. In addition to the underlying philosophical issues, it is arguable that in a domain such as business and management research, where there is an applied facet to some of the work, then invention, in the sense of forming new arrangements that may work, is an important activity as well as

15

discovery, in the sense of an attempt to portray what is happening.

In these terms the modest goal of this volume is to delineate the main claims to MM change, both as discoveries and inventions, in the domain of management theory discourse, and to assess the extent to which these changes are constructed and enacted in managerial and organizational settings.

PRESENTATION OF THIS BOOK

The book will not address all the problems raised in the literature overview, but will focus on three main questions:

1 What are the changes if any experienced in Europe in MMs roles? What can be really observed?
2 In what kinds of organizational and managerial processes are these MMs involved? What policies senior executives of these organizations are implementing, if any, to change MMs roles, when they think it is necessary?
3 What are the reactions, attitudes and strategies adopted by MMs confronted with new role expectations?

In order to help the reader, we have indicated in Table 1.1 the main contribution of each chapter (except the first two) alongside the three questions.

The first part of the book is composed of two general chapters. F. Bournois and Y.-F. Livian compare the titles and definitions given to the managerial population by different European countries, for example managers in the UK, 'cadres' in France and *'leitende angestellte'* in Germany. Their analysis in Chapter 2 has a practical purpose if we want to progress with a better understanding of European realities. But the chapter suggests also that, beyond translation problems, what is at stake is the

Table 1.1 Chapters contributing to the three main questions

Questions	Chapters								
	3	4	5	6	7	8	9	10	11
What changes if any?		X		X	X			X	
What processes and policies?	X					X	X		
What reactions and attitudes?			X			X		X	X

historical and social process by which social categories are constructed in different institutional environments.

Starting from theoretical debates in organization studies and choosing a social constructionist view, M. Van Gils shows in Chapter 3 that managerial functions are essentially discursive, in the way that it is through communication and dialogue, that new meanings are created and through which there is an ongoing process of organizing. This MM communication role has been seen, in the managerial literature as a rational behaviour aimed at motivating subordinates. Van Gils thinks that a better view is to consider the manager as providing an intelligible formulation of problems. Managers' skills are primarily in the area of 'problem setting', even more than in problem-solving. In change situations, a creation of new meanings is needed, and this happens only through language. It is the reason why MMs play a vital role in change: they are the people who can create these meanings in the ongoing process of communication.

With Chapter 4, we turn to empirical studies about MM in different parts of the European Union (EU). J. Burgoyne, F. Vouzas and Y.-F. Livian provide a comparative analysis of five countries involved in our programme, based on interviews in fifteen organizations (two private industrial companies and one general hospital per country). Starting from the hypotheses found in the literature, this survey shows that changes affecting MM roles may have been exaggerated, and provides a general picture more stable than could have been expected: throughout the different companies in the fifteen countries, there are very few radical organizational changes, which may transform completely MM roles. Middle managers have still very often a strict operational role constrained by organizational rules and business objectives. In small companies with family-style management, MMs are keeping a hierarchical role and are expected to show strong loyalty. Some larger organizations, specially in the UK and The Netherlands, have a more organic style and are implementing decentralization policies. But globally MMs are rarely involved in the strategy formation, and often feel an increasing pressure and stress. Middle managers are experiencing more change in the health sector, due to recent decentralization and cost reduction policies. A common evolution is the development of expectations about people-oriented skills, but knowing that the training and development programmes aimed at helping these managers to acquire them are infrequently available.

J.-P. Segal's chapter is based on extensive studies on MM in large public companies in France. The diagnosis often made by senior executives ('we have a MM problem') is discussed, and the views of the different actors on each other are analysed. For the author, looking at the so-called 'MM problems' is a revelation of the general disfunctions and paradoxes experienced by the organization. Chapter 4 examines the different reactions of MMs to these situations and shows how they vary according to the career stage MMs have reached. It questions the current view about MMs being reluctant to change and explains why, when it is true, other explanations than mere 'archaism' or 'bad temper' must be found.

The view of S. Kufidu, E. Petridu and D.M. Mihail is also based on field study in the public sector, this time in administrative offices. Chapter 6 reveals that, contrary to the claimed evolution due to a changing environment, the MM work in Greek public services is still mainly devoted to routine administrative tasks. In this context, MMs have a very limited authority and their real influence on HRM is very low. A majority of them would like to evolve towards what the authors call 'modern' roles, but the MMs seem not to be encouraged and supported to succeed in this change, in spite of the institutional reforms which are presently ongoing.

H.H. Larsen's chapter develops the idea of a growing HRM role for MMs in Denmark but shows also the paradoxical nature of a situation where, at the same time, delayering causes MMs to disappear. Chapter 7 presents three Danish cases, in which the position and roles of MMs are strikingly different: one 'revolutionary' company having experienced a radical transformation which induced a suppression of intermediate levels; a bureaucratic organization trying to develop management skills for its MMs and a third one having suppressed and reintroduced a level of MMs.

Most of the empirical data included in this book have analysed middle management levels and not specifically foremen and supervisors. But it would have been a pity not to deal with the evolutions affecting these groups in Europe, and above all the general trend of hiring 'new' foremen holding a higher training level. In Chapter 8 P. Trouve presents the results of a large study focused on foremen in French companies, and especially the 'new' generation having a better level of education. They are younger than their colleagues. They have reached line management positions faster. They have long been awaited by managers and executives who dreamt of replacing 'traditional' foremen. However, the 'new' generation have not provided all the benefits and virtues that were expected from them: their expectations frequently have not been fulfilled in their companies, and the pace of organizational change has been much slower than envisaged.

F. Vouzas, using the empirical data presented in Chapter 4, focuses in Chapter 9 on quality management and its impact on MMs. He shows that there are, among the organizations studied, four different stages of quality management, from the recent creation of a specific function to an overall project of implementing the core principles of TQM. The situations of MMs are quite different in these stages. After the quality circles phase, where a strong resistance from MMs has been shown, the involvement of these managers has been increasing. All the private organizations visited had the ISO 9000 certification, and very often MMs played a vital role in elaborating and enforcing the new procedures. In these cases, certification has been an opportunity for MMs to develop, or regain, organizational influence. TQM is perceived more as a fashionable system promoted by senior executives, without direct impact on MMs.

S. Dopson, Jean Neumann and Helen Newell's chapter is based on an extensive survey of 500 MMs in British companies and analyses the changes affecting MMs using for this the 'psychological contract' perspective. In their view, there are a large number of elements to these contracts which are presently under profound change. They identify three types of negative reactions of managers corresponding to different stages of their career.

In Chapter 11 M. Rousselot presents the point of view of someone who is at the same time an observer of the evolutions of European managerial staff, and an actor as president of a union organization at EU level. He is convinced that managerial staff have been confronted with critical changes but is confident of their ability to cope with the changes. He thinks that this group is strongly in favour of European construction but highlights different stakes for the future, specially the European recognition of qualifications and the development of a 'European model' of management.

Finally an overall conclusion, pinpointing convergences, is drawn.

NOTES

1 Official categories specified by the INSEE (Institut National de la Statistique et des Etudes Economiques).
2 We will see in Chapter 11 that the European group of unions speak of P and MS 'professional and managerial staff'.
3 We will use extensively for that purpose a literature survey prepared by F. Vouzas under the supervision of Professor Burgoyne.

REFERENCES

Ackroyd, S. (1992) 'Paradigms lost: paradise regained?', In M.I. Reed and M. Hugues (eds) *Rethinking Organizations: New Directions in Organization Theory and Analysis*, London: Sage, 102–19.

Alvesson, M. and Willmott, H. (1992) 'On the idea of emancipation in management and organizations studies', *Harvard Business Review*, November–December: 136.

Applegate, L.M., Cash, J.I and Mills, D.Q. (1988) 'Information technology and tomorrow's managers', *Harvard Business Review*, November–December: 136.

Aubert, N. and De Gaulejac, V. (1991) *Le coût de l'excellence*, Paris: Seuil.

Barry, T. (1992) 'The manager as a coach', *Industrial and Commercial Training*.

Beer, M., Spector, B., Lawrence, P., Quinn Mills, D. and Walton, R.E. (1984) *Managing Human Assets*, New York: Free Press.

Berger, P. And Luckman, T. (1966) The Social Construction of Reality, Harmondsworth: Penguin.

Breen, E.G. (1984) *Middle Management Morale in the 1980s*, American Management Association Survey Report.

Brennan, M. (1991) 'Mismanagement and quality circles: how middle managers influence direct participation', *Employee Relations* 13(5): 22–32.

Burgelman, R.A. (1983) 'Corporate entrepreneurship and strategic management: insights from a process study', *Management Science* 7(29):1349–64.

Burgoyne, J.G. (1994) 'Stakeholder analysis', in C. Cassel and G. Symon (eds) *Qualitative Methods in Organizational and Occupational Psychology*, London: Sage

Burgoyne, J.G. and Lorbiecki, A. (1993) 'Clinicians into Management: the experience in context', *Health Services Management Research* 6(4): 248–59.

Burgoyne, J.G., Pedler, M. and Boydell, T. (eds) (1994) *Towards the Learning Company: Concepts and Practices*, Maidenhead: McGraw-Hill.

Carr, C. (1987), 'Injecting quality into Personnel Management', *Personnel Journal*, September: 43–51.

Chia, R. (1994), 'Management research as academic entrepreneurship: towards the craft of imaginative knowledging, working paper presented at the British Academy of Management Conference, Lancaster University, 12–14 September. Abstract in Westall, O. (ed.) (1994), *British Academy of Management 1994 Annual Conference Proceedings*, Lancaster: The Management School, Lancaster University.

Collard, R. (1989) *Total Quality: Success through People*, Wimbledon: IPM.

Crosby, P.B. (1979) *Quality is Free*, New York: McGraw-Hill.

Dany, F. and Livian, Y.-F. (1995) *La gestion des cadres*, Paris: Vuibert.

Darwent, C. (1991) 'Management today, 25th anniversary', *Management Today*, 25 November.

Deming, W.E. (1986) *Out of the Crisis*, Cambridge: Cambridge University Press.

D'Iribarne, A. (1989) *La compétitivité: enjeu social et éducatif*, Paris: CNRS.

Donaldson, L. (1985) 'Entrepreneurship applied to middle management', *Journal of General Management* 10(4).

Dopson, S. (1992) 'Middle managers pivotal role', *Management Development Review* 5(5): 8–11.

Dopson, S. and Stewart, R. (1992) 'The changing role of the middle manager in the UK', *International Studies of Management and Organization* 22(1): 40–53.

— (1993) 'Information technology, organizational restructuring and the future of middle management', *New Technology, Work and Employment* 8(1):10–20.

Drucker, P.F. (1970) *Drucker on Management*, London: Management Publications Limited for the British Institute of Management, 165.

— (1980) *Managing in Turbulent Times*, New York: Harper and Row.

— (1988) 'The coming of the new organization', *Harvard Business Review*, January–February: 45–53.

Dunaine, B. (1993), 'The non-managers', *Fortune* 127(4): 38–42.

Eberwein, W. and Tholen, J (1993) *Euromanager or splendid isolation? International Management: An Anglo-German Comparison*, Berlin: De Gruyter.

Eccles, T. (1994) *Succeeding with Change*, Maidenhead: McGraw-Hill.

Fineman, S. (1983) *White Collar Unemployment: Impact and Stress*, London: Wiley, 154.

Fox S. (1992) 'The European learning community: towards a political economy of management learning', *Human Resource Management Journal* 3(1).

Foy, N. (1981) *The Yin and Yang of Organizations*, New York: William Morrow.

Gotlieb L. (1990), 'Survival strategies for middle managers', *Business Quarterly*, Summer: 118–22.

Handy, C.B. (1991) *Gods of Management: The Changing Work of Organisations*, 3rd edn, London: Business Books, 250.

Handy, C., Gow I., Gordon, C., Randelsome, C. and Maloney, M. (1987) *The Making of Managers*, London: National Economic Development Office.

21

Hicks, R.L. (1971) 'Developing the top management group in a total systems organization', *Personnel Journal* **50**(9): 675–682.

Hills, S. (1991) 'Why quality circles failed but total quality management might succeed', *British Journal of Industrial Relations* **29**(9): 675–682.

Hofstede, G. (1980) *Culture's Consequences*, Beverly Hills, CA: Sage.

Horne, J.H. and Lupton, T. (1965) 'The work activities of middle managers', *Journal of Management Studies* **2**: 14–33

Inkson, K. and Coe, T. (1992) *Are Career Ladders Disappearing?* Corby: The Institute of Management, University of Auckland.

Ishikawa, K. (1985) *What Is TQC? The Japanese Way*, Englewood Cliffs, NJ: Prentice Hall.

Juran, J.M. (1988) *Quality Control Handbook*, New York: McGraw-Hill.

Kanter R.M. (1982), 'The middle manager as innovator', *Harvard Business Review*, July–August.

— (1986) 'The reshaping of middle management', *Management Review*, January, 19–20.

Kanter, R.M. and Stein B. (1979) *Life in Organizations*, New York: Basic Books.

Kay, E. (1974) 'Middle management', in J. O'Toole (ed.), *Work and the Quality of Life*, Cambridge, MA: MIT Press.

Klemp, G.O. Jr and McClelland, D.C. (1986) 'What characterizes intelligent functioning among senior managers?' in R.J. Sternberg and R.K. Wagner (eds), *Practical Intelligence*, Cambridge: Cambridge University Press.

Kotter, J. (1982) *The General Manager*, New York: Free Press.

Kravetz, D.J. (1988) *The Human Management Revolution*, San Francisco: Jossey Bass.

Kurke, L.B. and Aldrich, H.E. (1983) 'Mintzberg was right', *Management Science*, **29**(8), August: 975–84.

Leavitt, H. (1986) *Corporate Pathfinders*, Homewood: Irwin.

Leavitt, H. and Whistler, L. (1964), 'Manager in the 1980s', in: Leavitt, H. and Pondy, L.R. (eds) *Readings in Managerial Psychology*, Chicago: University of Chicago Press, 578–92.

Levine, H.Z. (1986) 'The squeeze of middle management', *Personnel* **63**(1), January: 62–9.

Luthans, F. and Lockwood, D.L. (1984) 'Towards an observation systems for measuring leader behavior,' in Hunt, J.G., Hosking, D.M., Schriesheim, C.A., and Stewart, R. (eds) *Leaders and Managers*, New York: Pergamon.

McDermont, L. (1992) *Caught up in the Middle*, Englewood Cliffs, NJ: Prentice Hall.

Marshall, J. and Cooper, C.L. (1977) 'Work experiences of middle and senior managers', *Management International Review*, **19**: 81–96.

Mintzberg, H. (1973) *The Nature of Managerial Work*, New York: Harper and Row.

— (1994) *The Rise and Fall of Strategic Planning*, New York: Prentice Hall.

Mitroff, L.L. and Bennis, W. (1993) 'The unreality industry', *The Deliberate Manufacture of Falsehood and What It Is Doing to our Lives*, Oxford: Oxford University Press.

Morgan, G. (1988) *Riding the Waves of Change. Developing Managerial Competencies for a Turbulent World*, San Francisco: Jossey-Bass.

Neumann, P. (1978) 'What speed of communication is doing to span of control', *Administrative Management*, **39**(11): 30–46.

Nicholson, N. and West, M. (1988) *Managerial Job Change*, Cambridge: Cambridge University Press.

Nonaka, I. (1988) 'Towards middle-up down management: accelerating information creation', *Sloan Management Review*, Spring (88): 9–18.

Pedler, M.J., Burgoyne, J.G. and Boydell, T. (1991) *The Learning Company: A Strategy for Sustainable Development*, Maidenhead: McGraw-Hill.

Pettigrew, A.M. (ed.) (1988) *Competitiveness and the Management Process*, Oxford: Blackwell.

Pinsonneault, A. and Kraemer, K. (1993) 'The impact of information technology on middle managers', *MIS Quarterly*, September.

Plowman B. (1992) 'A role for managers in total quality', in: M. Hand and B. Plowman (eds), *Quality Management Handbook*, Oxford: Butterworth-Heinemann.

Polakoff, J.C. (1987) 'Will middle managers work in the factory of the future?', *Management Review*, **26**(1): 50–1.

Popper, K.R. (1963) *Conjectures and Refutations: the Growth of Scientific Knowledge*, London: Routledge, 412.

Reed, M. (1989) *The Sociology of Management*, Hemel Hempstead: Harvester Wheatsheaf.

Roomkin, M. (1991) 'The changing characteristics of managers and managerial employment in the 1980s', in *International Comparisons in Human Resource Management*, C. Brewster and C. Tyson (eds) London: Pitman.

Sayles L. (1964) *Managerial Behavior*, New York: McGraw-Hill.

Schilit, W.K. (1987) 'An examination of the influence of middle-level manager in formulating and implementing strategic decisions', *Journal of Management Studies* **24**: 271–93.

Silverman D. (1970) *The Theory of Organizations*, London: Heinemann.

Smits, S.J. (1989) 'Middle managers: coping with the "natural state"', *Training and Development*, March: 65–7.

Stewart, R. (1967) *Managers and their Jobs*, Maidenhead: McGraw-Hill.

— (1982) *Choices for the Manager*, Englewood Cliff, NJ: Prentice Hall.

— (1991) *Managing Today and Tomorrow*, London: MacMillan.

— (1993a) *Handbook of Management Skills*, Aldershot: Gower.

— (1993b) 'Performance Management'. *Benefits and Compensation International* **23**(1): 20–21.

Storey, J. (1992) *Developments in the Management of Human Resources*, Oxford: Blackwell.

Taddei, D. and Coriat, B. (1993) *Made in France*, Paris: Livre de Poche.

Torrington, D. and Weightman, J. (1987) 'Middle management work', *Journal of General Management* **13**(2): 74–89.

Weiss, R. (1988) 'Will the role of managers decline in the corporation of the future?', *National Productivity Review* **7**(2): 114–121.

Westley, F.R. (1990) 'Middle managers and strategy: microdynamics of inclusion', *Strategic Management Journal* **11**: 337–51.

Wilkinson, A., Redman, T. and Snape, E. (1993) *Quality and the Manager*, Corby: Institute of Management.

Wisdom, B.L. and Benton, D.K. (1992) 'Manager as a teacher', *Training and Development*.

Wooldridge, B. and Floyd, S.W. (1990) 'The strategy process, middle management involvement, and organizational performance', *Strategic Management Journal* **11**: 231–41.

Zarifian, P. (1993) *Quel modèle d'organisation pour l'industrie européenne?* Paris: L'Harmattan.

Zemke, R. (1988) 'Putting the squeeze on middle managers', *Training* **25**(12): 41–46.

2

MANAGERS, 'CADRES', 'LEITENDE ANGESTELLTE'

Some landmarks about managerial group titles and definitions

Frank Bournois and Yves-Frédéric Livian

INTRODUCTION

'Managers', 'cadres', *'leitende Angestellte'*: beyond the words themselves and their translation into other European languages, the very definition of this group raises the problem of comparing countries that have different social and organizational structures. It is noticeable that most of the recent books about HRM in Europe avoid the topic of analysing and comparing social and occupational groups. Without wishing to give an exhaustive picture of this difficult question, we would like to provide, as an introductory topic, some indications of the position of the managerial group within this European diversity.[1] Our objectives are to give a description of the categorization existing in various European countries, and to propose some adequate interpretations.

TOWARDS AN INTERNATIONAL DEFINITION OF THE NOTION OF 'MANAGER'?

It is not easy to even propose an international definition of a manager. After the tripartite meeting of the International Labour Organization (ILO) at Geneva in November 1977, a summary of the 'principles and good practices relating to the employment of professional workers' was established, which provides the first international definition of professional or managerial workers:

> Any person: (a) who has completed a professional training and education at a higher level or who possesses an

25

equivalent recognised experience in a scientific, technical, administrative domain, and (b) who carries out, as a paid employee, functions of predominantly an intellectual nature, comprising the application at a high level of the faculties of judgment and initiative, and entailing a relatively high level of responsibility. This notion also includes any person meeting the characteristics (a) and (b) above who is invested by delegation from the employer and under his authority, with the responsibility of planning, directing, checking, and coordinating the activities of a part of a company or an organization, with the commensurate power of command, including executives. The term does not cover top-level managers who have a large delegation of authority from their employers.

(Bournois, 1990: 87)

This definition helps to highlight the five dimensions that we can use to specify what is a 'managerial' group of jobs:

- level of education and/or the level of experience
- salaried condition
- intellectual nature of work
- delegation received from the employer
- responsibility of 'managing' others.

It also raises some critical questions about European comparisons in this field:

1 Professional training and education on the one hand, and practical experience on the other: in each country, we find a combination of these two paths, giving access to managerial positions. But the quantitative importance of each one, and the level and type of positions accessible is likely to be influenced by the institutional context.

The reference to a 'recognition' of experience is also a dimension which can differentiate different contexts: for example French companies do not use officially recognized systems. Large-sized companies use specific formal systems of their own, when they want to promote a supervisor or technician to a managerial position. Custom and practice is also predominant in the UK, but there have been recent attempts to move to official systems (such as APL, (accreditation of prior learning) though the application is far from universal.

2 The reference to such behaviours as: 'initiative', 'responsibility', is certainly a common characteristic of 'managerial' positions. But their concrete implementation relies on organizational conditions and style of leadership, and the stress which is put on these behaviours is greatly determined by the context existing in the sector or in the country. We can observe very different conditions.[2]

3 If we try to differentiate 'managers' from other occupational groups, such as technicians and professionals, we can see that the three first dimensions are not able to provide a differentiation. As such, managers can be considered as 'knowledge workers', a category of growing interest from a sociological point of view.[3]

Managers share the fourth characteristic with supervisors, but also in a way with experts and professionals working in organizations. All are on the receiving end of delegation from the employer. On this point, we may observe not only national/institutional differentiations, but also differences as to how this delegation is given, recognized, accepted, formalized and controlled.

The responsibility of 'managing' others and the existence of power of command (even if it is given and exerted in different ways) remains the only dimension specific to management, and then only when it is combined with the dimensions relating to level of education and range of delegation received.[4]

In fact, these dimensions are building a basis on which some common traits can be noticed in Europe: the salaried condition, the nature of the task, the delegation received, the responsibility. It is this type of common ground which allows statistical studies about managers in Europe even if they must be read with caution. For example, a French study about 'Cadres' in Europe gives approx. 8.1 million of these people working in the EU, in private companies with more than ten employees. Out of 100 employees, twelve to thirteen are 'Cadres' on average. The 'managerial proportion' varies from 9.5 per cent in Germany to 16 per cent in Denmark, 15 per cent in the UK, and 14.5 per cent in Spain and France.[5] The International Standard Classification of Occupations (ISCO) figures (see Table 2.1) show a different approach, distinguishing 'professionals and managers' from 'technicians and associate professionals' and covering all the sectors. The average

Table 2.1 Total employment in twelve European countries

	Total employees (m.)	Professionals and managers ISCO 1—2		Technicians and associate professionals ISCO 3		Other employees ISCO 4—9	
		Employees	%	Employees	%	Employees	%
Belgium	3.1	0.7	22	0.3	10	2.1	68
Denmark	2.4	0.4	17	0.4	17	1.6	66
France	18.7	2.6	14	3.3	18	12.8	68
Germany	35.9	4.3	13	5.9	18	22.7	69
Greece	1.9	0.4	21	0.2	11	1.3	68
Ireland	0.9	0.2	22	0.1	11	0.6	67
Italy	14.9	1.6	11	1.9	13	11.4	76
Luxembourg	0.2	—	—	—	—	0.2	—
Netherlands	5.8	1.4	24	1.0	17	3.4	59
Portugal	3.4	0.3	9	0.4	12	2.7	79
Spain	9.1	1.2	13	0.4	4	7.5	83
United Kingdom	22.1	6.0	27	1.7	8	14.4	65
Totals for 12 countries	115.4	19.1	16	15.6	14	80.7	70

Source: EUROCADRES: figures EUROSTAT, Labour Force Survey 1992

Note: ISCO = International Standard Classification of Occupations (published 1988)

rate for EU is 16 per cent (19 million people out of 115.4 million employees). The proportion of professional and managerial staff varies from 9 per cent in Portugal to 27 per cent in the UK. But it is much more risky to propose comparative figures about the sub-groups inside the overall 'managers' category.

The level of education and/or experience is, on the contrary, a dimension in which we will find a wide range of situations, sometimes within the same country. We have here a good example of the link between organizational structures and educational systems. In Germany for example, different levels of educational background seem to provide 'managers' at different hierarchical levels but with some flexibility. The internal promotion system is very active, with a strong emphasis on professional experience. Also, there is high social recognition for technical expertise, creating a common frame of reference. However, in France the diploma plays a greater role. Big companies hire preferably young graduates and are reluctant to appoint as middle managers people having only technical training or no degree at all, even with substantial experience and good results.

Even with this variety of educational background, and the balance that every system makes between formal training and experience, the ILO definition depicts a group of salaried people inside of which other distinctions must be made. These distinctions must be based on two elements:

- the level of responsibility, or the level in the hierarchy, which vary depending on the organizational levels used by the companies[6]
- the social norms existing in the local business culture, giving symbolic meaning to distinctions inside the managerial group.

DIFFERENCES WITHIN EUROPE

We here present some of the distinctions among several European countries.[7]

In France the notion of 'cadre' corresponds in the first instance to an institutionalized category. 'Cadres' are agents with technical, administrative, legal, commercial or financial training to whom the employer has delegated significant authority over co-workers of every type: blue-collar workers, white-collar workers, technicians, foremen and forewomen, administrative or commercial workers. They are supposed to have a relatively high degree of responsibility. In France, 'cadres' are often educated in the university system or in the system of the prestigious *grandes écoles*, which allows graduates to be directly recruited as 'cadres' in companies. There is a clear-cut distinction between the status of 'Cadre' (specific retirement systems, higher social status) and that of the other workers, even those having some kind of managerial responsibility (for example, supervisors).

The staff of a company is composed of blue-collar workers ('ouvriers'), white-collar workers ('employés'), technicians and foremen ('techniciens et agents de maîtrise'), and engineers and managers ('cadres'). Sometimes, 'employés', 'techniciens' et 'agents de maîtrise' are grouped under the acronym 'ETAM'. There can be three main categories (workers, ETAM and cadres) or even two – 'cadres' and 'non cadres' (non-managers). Engineers and managers are ruled by specific collective agreements in several sectors.

In Italy, the Italian civil code provides four socio-professional categories: blue-collar workers (*operai*), white-collar workers (*impiegati*), middle-level managers (*quadri*), and upper level (*dirigenti*). The emergence of the 'middle managers' group has been the consequence of an industrial conflict in 1985. Collective agreements define who are *quadri* and *dirigenti*. It is interesting to notice that the definition of '*quadri*' relies on the notion of 'continuous' function 'having a strong impact for corporate growth . . .' The *dirigenti* are defined only by 'a role characterized by a high level of professional competence' (Bournois, 1990: 87).

In Germany, the essential distinction is between blue-collar workers and white-collar workers. In the national statistics, the white-collar workers ('angestellte') are a large group, composed of all people who are not blue-collar workers, working in organized professions or owners of their industry or shop.[8] Within this group, the fact of distinguishing 'superior' employees is a recent phenomenon (the 1970s), and is more an internal classification in companies rather than a social group or class. Among the white-collar workers, there are those who are covered by collective agreements (*tariffliche Angestellte*), and those who are not (*aussertariffliche Angestellte*).[9] If we take the German structure from top to the bottom, the following distinctions are made:

1. Top management (*Vorstandmitglieder*) and members of the board (*Vorstand*).
2. *Leitende Angestellte*, who are managerial personnel and not part of collective agreements (the unions are reluctant to use this notion).
3. *Aussertariffliche Angestellte*, among whom are the *Bereichsleiter* (section heads), *Hauptabteilungsleiter* (heads of large departments), and some *Abteilungsleiter* (department heads).
4. The first-level personnel (*Tariffliche Angestellte*). Only a small number of them can lay claim to the title of manager; these are a few *Abteilungsleiter* (department heads) and engineers in a staff position (without authority). A developing term covering the 'cadres' population is also 'Fach und Fürhungskräfte'

In the UK there are no legal provisions defining the concept of 'manager'. The term 'manager' is very broad and covers several types of responsibility. As the report of the ILO also points out, the notion of manager has a tendency to include foremen and forewomen. We can retain the following categories, which are the product of professional practice:

- top managers and directors
- senior managers
- middle managers
- junior managers
- supervisory managers.

The Institute of Management, a professional association, seems to deplore the large number of persons who avail themselves of the title 'manager' and whom the Institute do not recognize. The Management Charter Initiative, having established standards for all managerial positions, distinguishes four levels:

- senior managers
- middle managers
- first-line managers
- supervisory managers.

In the Netherlands, there is a difference between managers who are covered by collective agreements and managers not covered by these agreements. In general young graduates from the university or 'Hoge School' (bachelor degree level) may start with salaries based on a collective agreement but they are not obliged to. However, there is not a strong demarcation. This category is labelled 'junior managers'.

The term '*Kader*' has been used for those managers (often labelled as '*baas*' (boss) who have no higher education degree and whose salary level is covered by collective agreements. Their promotion chances are in general within the terms of the collective agreement. The term '*kader*' is rarely used any more except in the Flemish part of Belgium. The concept of *baas* comes close to 'first-line supervisor'.

The term '*bestuurder*' is used in relation to the top management of large multidivisional firms (member of the *raad van bestuur*) and has a legal connotation. Below the level of a *raad van bestuur* one finds the directors of divisions, business units, etc. Below the 'directors' one finds the 'senior managers'. Below the 'senior managers' (in large firms) one finds the middle managers, often indicated as 'head of . . . '.

Dutch managerial structure has been highly influenced by the German tradition, but after the Second World War, when the number of academically qualified managers increased rapidly (in the 1950s only 3 per cent had an academic degree), has moved (in language) towards the Anglo-Saxon tradition.

In Spain, the legal context is not developed on this point and the concept covers a variety of functions ranging from general manager to head of sales. Two categories of 'cadres' are generally distinguished: the *Gerente* (managerial people specified by Article 2 of Decree 1382 of 1985, concerning the labour contract) and the *Cuadros* (other people). In organizations, these managers can be split into two levels: *'jefe'* (chief) and 'deputy chief'.

In Belgium, which follows a logic similar to that used in France, the term cadres is used, the equivalent in Flemish being *kader, bestuurder, beheerder* and *leider*.

In Greece, the term 'manager' has no legal status and its meaning is very broad. Practically the person who acts as manager may cover several types of responsibilties depending on the company's policy. Only the 'general Director' and 'Directors' are distinguished by corporate law. From the legal point of view the term 'directors' refers only to persons who are officially authorized by the company to take and implement decisions closely connected with the company's development.

In Portugal, there are several ways to translate the term 'manager'. The best is probably the term *'gestor'*, used to refer to top or senior management or persons who have diplomas from management schools. The term *'director'* is also used in the national classification of professions (Administradores e directores gerais). Finally, the term *'gerente'* is also used, mostly in small and medium-sized firms, whose legal duties are specified in the commercial code. The term *'quadro'* is also developing.

In Switzerland, the German term *kader*, derived from military terminology (as in France), is quite specific. The Swiss are very attached to their reserve army, to which reservists belong throughout their entire adult life. There are some extremely strong bridges between the army and the company, so much so that there is a corresponding strong parallelism between military rank and hierarchical position in a company. To obtain evidence of this, it is sufficient to count the number of managers of Swiss banks who are colonels in the Swiss army.

We summarize and compare the different groups and subgroups in the managerial population in the Figure 2.1. In this figure, we have tried to design a line defining levels of

MANAGERIAL GROUP TITLES AND DEFINITIONS

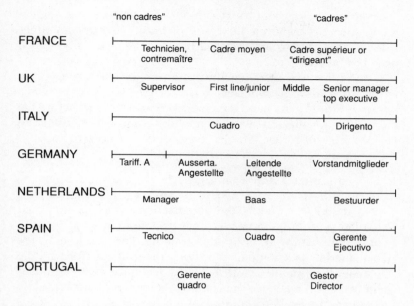

Figure 2.1 Comparison of European managerial group structures: a floating frontier in a borderless Europe

responsibility (from the lower level at the left, to the higher at the right). Outside the extreme left part of our line, medium or low-level white-collar employees, and blue-collar workers (technical staff are not considered, except in the case of France). At the end of the line, at the right, are CEOs. We have designed the *de facto* barrier to career progression existing in France between the 'cadres' and 'non-managers'. Without comparing the barrier, which seems to have different meanings, we have also represented the delineation existing in Italy (the two groups) and Germany (those people covered by a collective agreement and those who are not).

Most of the countries use different terms but have a continuum rather than clear frontiers inside the managerial group, France being an exception. Most of them have different terms mainly for distinguishing senior level, or executive, and the others. Even if they are salaried people, the responsibilities, rights and duties of senior managers are different from other managers in Italy, for example. In this country, they have a specific collective agreement. Also, separation is the result of traditions but sometimes formalized by law rules. It is clearly a social construction which needs to be analysed.

A good theoretical framework for analysing these differences is the 'societal approach' developed by the Aix Group. In this approach, three macro-social elements contribute to structure the organization, through worker mobility and distribution in various job categories. At their turn, policies and structures of the companies influence societal context.[10]

1 The educational and training system, which provides the economic system with people having certain qualifications, contributes to structure the organization, which is supposed to offer positions adapted to the expectations and background of people having received this training. For example, in the managerial population, the type of training for middle managers (apprenticeship vs formal, technical vs general) and the type of positions available in companies are strongly linked. This explains many of the differences between social systems. In their famous comparison between Germany and France, Maurice et al. (1982) show that engineers and managers in France hold a high status, largely on the basis of a previous selection by the grandes écoles system. The supervisors have often a low-level qualification, technical vocational training having in France low social recognition. This social and symbolic distance between the two groups creates difficulty for communication. In the German case a common language, technical expertise, unites different organizational levels. Technical training is highly respected (see Figure 2.2). Of course, the educational system is in turn affected by companies' employment policies.

2 The organizational system, which creates continuities or discontinuities in the hierarchical scale, and which facilitates or hinders co-operation between units and services, has a strong impact on the structure of managerial positions. In weak hierarchical systems there is a short distance, for example, between middle managers and supervisors, creating a homogeneous professional space. In more stratified systems there is a need for designing and managing different groups, which in fact have few possibilities of mobility.

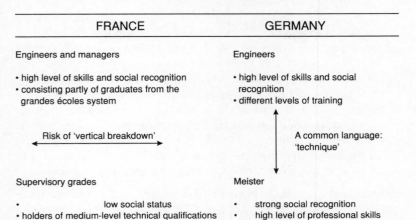

FRANCE	GERMANY
Engineers and managers	Engineers
• high level of skills and social recognition • consisting partly of graduates from the grandes écoles system	• high level of skills and social recognition • different levels of training

Risk of 'vertical breakdown'

A common language: 'technique'

Supervisory grades	Meister
• low social status • holders of medium-level technical qualifications	• strong social recognition • high level of professional skills • legitimate authority

Figure 2.2 Comparison of the managerial system in France and Germany
Source: Adapted from Maurice, Sellier and Silvestre (1982)

The interaction and feedback between the education systems and organization systems creates paths of access to functions and positions. A good example is given in the case of comparative studies about engineers, and specially Lanciano et al.'s (1992) research about innovation in France and Japan. The authors show that, in France, the title of 'engineer' and the 'cadre' status provide rapidly a recognized position and a starting-point for a career. In Japan, young graduates become engineers after a long-lasting process within the company through functional mobility and development of a collective knowledge. The intermediate group of 'technicians', which in France groups people having short technical training, and whose function is to implement technical decisions or to operate equipment, do not exist in Japanese companies. These tasks are done by young engineers, at the beginning of their career. We can see in this case that the very existence of a social and occupational group is determined by a specific type of organizational/educational interaction.

3 The industrial relations system establishes the type of relations between employers, public bodies and unions. In the

35

case of management populations, this system may have a weaker impact than for the worker groups. It can be said that, originally, the manager was defined by the fact that he or she was not part of any professional hierarchy (out of the tariff, as we have seen for Germany) (Eyraud and Rozenblatt, 1994). But again, institutional arrangements may differ from one country to another in terms of whether managers are a recognized group, hold specific rights, and are subjected to specific employment contracts. The study of the position of this group in the larger negotiation system would be a very fruitful way of comparing these groups from one context to another.

These ideas are only hypotheses drawn from a stimulating theoretical framework, not yet specifically applied to the managerial group. But we are convinced that it could provide a rich path towards a systematic analysis of European managerial realities.

CONCLUSION

In conclusion, we have seen that:

1 Research is not well advanced in the field of European comparisons of social and occupational groups. However, a clear vision of definitions given in each country and the meaning of the titles and positions used is required for a better understanding of HRM in Europe.
2 There are few dimensions which help to define 'managerial' groups of jobs, if we look at this reality from the point of view of job analysis and organization functioning. We can see these groups as knowledge workers having significant delegation from the employer and holding a power of command.
3 Our comparison shows that some countries have legal or contractual specifications about these groups (France, Germany, Spain, Portugal, also Scandinavian countries). The only common characteristic is that all the countries studied are making a distinction at the upper level of decision-makers. However, the borders at the lower level, between middle management jobs and supervision jobs are not well specified, except in France (with the 'cadre' notion) and in UK in the latter's recent attempts to clarify managerial competencies.
4 The borders distinguishing several social categories are socially constructed. Professional categories are the product of

36

a very long historical process (Desrosières and Thevenot, 1988). In order to study this social construction, we need a large framework of analysis, taking into account not only organizational characteristics of each country, but also the institutional context (educational structures and industrial rules).

NOTES

1 We have used in this chapter a part of a former paper by F. Bournois (1992) 'The impact of 93 on Management Development in Europe' in *International Studies of Management and Organisation* R. Stewart (ed.) vol. no. 22 1. Thanks to Professors Van Gils, Kufidu and Mrs Proença, for their help about their countries and also to M. Rousselot for his helpful comments.
2 Chapters 6 and 7 of this book show contrasted examples.
3 See for example: Blackler F., Reed M., Whitaker A. (1993) 'Knowledge Workers and Contemporary Organisations', *Journal of Management Studies* **30**, November.
4 These three dimensions must be examined together if we want to distinguish – sometimes very difficult – 'middle managers' from other intermediate occupations, such as foremen, supervisors etc.
5 'Cadroscope' in 'Courrier Cadres', APEC, 1032, October 1993. 'Cadres' are defined as 'salaried people having either large technical responsibilities, or command of people'.
6 This means that the 'lean', or 'delayered' structure, often depicted as the future of organizations in post-industrialized countries, will have less possibilities of differentiating subgroups and categories. One could answer that there is no longer a need for differentiation. But is HRM, at least in large organizations, other than a rationalized way of ranking people?
7 See the ILO report on this topic about five countries (Italy, Germany, France, UK and Sweden), Geneva, 1986.
8 Forty-one per cent of active population in 1987. See, on this topic, B. Krais (1992)
9 'Tariffliche' meaning 'collective agreement'; '*angestellte*' for employee; aussertariffliche: out of collective agreement.
10 See M. Maurice, F. Sellier and J.J. Silvestre. (1984) 'The search for a societal effect in the production of hierarchy: a comparison of France and Germany' in *Internal Labour Markets*, P. Osterman (ed.) Cambridge MA: MIT Press.

REFERENCES

Bournois, F. (1990) 'Europeanization des grandes enterprises et gestion des cadres', PhD dissertation, Université Lyon 3.
Bournois, F. (1991) *La gestion des cadres en Europe*, Paris: Eyrolles.

Desrosières, A. and Thevenot L. (1988) *Les catégories socio-professionnelles*, Paris: La Découverte.

Eyraud, F. and Rozenblatt, P. (1994) *Les formes hiérarchiques: travail et salaires dans 9 pays industrialisés*, Paris: La Documentation Française.

Krais, B., (1992) Pourquoi n'y a-t-il pas de 'cadres' en Allemagne? *Sociologie du Travail*, 4.

Lanciano, C., Maurice, M., Nohara, H. and Silvestre J.J. (1992) *Innovation: acteurs et organisations. Les ingénieurs et la dynamique de l'entreprise. Comparaison France–Japon*, Aix-en-Provence: LEST, CNRS.

Maurice, M., Sellier, F. and Silvestre J.J. (1982) *Politique d'éducation et organisation industrielle en France et en Allemagne*, Paris: PUF.

Osterman, P. (ed.) (1984) *Internal Labour Markets*, Cambridge, MA: MIT Press.

3

MIDDLE MANAGEMENT, COMMUNICATION AND ORGANIZATION CHANGE

Maarten Rudolf Van Gils

> The change of practices cannot be obtained by the trans-
> plantation, the addition or the accumulation of managerial
> novelties. It necessitates a deconstruction and a reformula-
> tion of the logics on the spot.
>
> (Midler, 1993: 185).

INTRODUCTION

In organization theory the popularity of the concept of *organization change* reflects the uncertainties in many branches of
industry. Concepts such as total quality control, re-engineering,
empowerment, synergy, core competencies, benchmarking, team
management, etc. are introduced in organizations as answers to
enhance competitive opportunities.

Whatever the precise definitions of these concepts, they carry
with them the necessities and the rhetoric of organization
change. Changes, as new concepts, have as their primary function not only to restructure and revitalize the organization and
to create for the company a prominent place in the market, but
also to emphasize the symbolic necessity that life in the company
should be different from what it is now. In change processes
middle management plays a vital communicative role. Yet at the
same time it is often argued that middle management is resistant
to change, that 'the buck stops'at middle management level, that
middle management is the 'clay' layer of the organization.

These qualifications of middle management more or less
suggest that there is an objective world of which representations

can be made, that knowledge can be built up that reflects or represents this world 'in itself', independent of the knower (Cooper, 1989; von Glasersfeld, 1981, 1984). The organization is a machine, therefore, and middle managers are the permanently available maintenance workers and repairers.

The statement that someone is resistant to change implies that there is an objective world which is unknown or denied by the receiver/listener. This 'modernist' view, often labelled as objective, centres around the idea that knowledge can be developed by systematically making representations of reality by making use of approved models of knowledge and rules of methodology. The field of organization theory is abundant with models which somehow suggest there is an objective world, that the implementation of specific models of change will lead to the desired results, will solve problems and therefore contribute to progress.

The modernist model is based upon the logocentric bias of steering from a fixed centre of origin; a centre that has the ability to control and make things more predictable (Cooper, 1989; Gergen, 1992; Sampson, 1989). Logocentrism can be defined as 'the belief in the possibility of full and perfect embodiment of thought in language, and the structures of repetition that guarantee it', but denies the situatedness in which language is placed (Connor, 1989: 139).

The paradox of the logocentric bias here is that not only change is necessary, but also the control of the change process. Change implies action, and action is never completely calculable. Change is by definition capricious. The question then arises what kind of control (financial, customers, human resources, etc.) is necessary in relation to the desired changes and to what extent is the change process supported by or thwarted by control measures. Further, who is responsible for the control of change processes and to what extent can those in charge of the daily business (middle management) be trusted to have the same ideas as those who can be considered as the initiators of change and those who have the final responsibility over actions taken?

Logocentrism is the assumption of the internal, reasoning agent with an emphasis on union of mind, thought and consciousness, and the structuralist thesis pretends that social practices, including the meaning of subject and subjectivity, are simply mediated by language; language therefore is conceived as a means for the communication of thoughts, as a carrier of representations of our world.

On the other hand there are the theories which are structured on the assumption that reality is a construction of the mind. Knowledge does not reflect an objective ontological reality, but exclusively an ordering and organization of the world by our experience. These theories are labelled as relativistic (Bernstein, 1983), subjective (Burrell and Morgan, 1979), endogenic (Gergen, 1982) or in its most extreme form as solipsism. This Cartesian either/or dualism between objectivism or relativism centres around the basic epistemological problem of how we can acquire knowledge of 'reality' and how 'reliable' and 'true' that knowledge might be.

The dichotomy *objectivism–relativism* has been the dominant characteristic of the field of organization studies and has exercised a tremendous influence on paradigm development. A paradigm development can be characterized as an 'epistemological odyssey': a continuous 'sailing between the scilla monster of representation and the charybdis whirlpool of solipsism' (Maturana and Varela, 1987: 134).

The manager who has or wants to have control, emphasizes primarily structure, neglects the essential communicative and other processual tasks essential in any management function and creates a *status quo* situation (Boland, et al., 1994; Cooper, 1989; Gergen, 1992; Sampson 1989;). Being in command creates easily the illusion of rationality, of absolute truth and, therefore, of having the power and the ability of steering from a fixed point of view. As Pinxten and Farber (1990) state, this being in command refers to the emphasis on norm and a context of truth, which makes paradoxes problematic and leads to avoidance, as it 'implies that there is one unique way that reality is and one unique way in which it should be rendered in the language of the learner' (also Shotter, 1993: 4). On the other hand the manager who lets things flow emphasizes action (processes), denies the importance of structure and loses control. A phenomenon well known in entrepreneurial management.

Against this classic dualism of either objectivism or relativism can be placed the model of understanding as discursive construction. Languaging in this model is a vital concept; language not as a system that represents, but language as a discourse. A discourse in which words gain their meaning primarily

41

by social interchange and in which words are context dependent.

In popular language the 'human mind', 'the individual' is commonly accepted as an object-like centre of awareness (Sampson, 1989), as the fundamental site of the production of meaning which suggests a representation of 'the world' and is communicated by language.

However, it is in communication, in dialogue, that new meanings are created and through which there is an ongoing process of organizing. Managerial functions are essentially discursive (Gergen, 1992) and are related to a process of organizing in which the interrelationship of both structure and action (process) are vital elements (Kilduff, 1993; Orlikowski and Yates, 1995).

It is therefore not only the dualistic either/or of making choices, of good or wrong, but also a both/and. The either/or implies that everything must either be or not be (Derrida, 1978). A both/and on the other hand implies the balancing of opposites, the recognition of the relationship between opposites, as opposites are defined in each other. There is no structure without process and no process without structure; there is no inside without outside and so on.

In this introduction a short presentation has been made concerning an epistemological debate in present organization theory. A debate that focuses on classical dualism (either/or) versus social constructivism (both/and). Mainstream theory is primarily based on dualism. This dualistic point of view in relation to middle management and its communicative role will be elaborated in the following two sections. In the final section middle management is approached from a social constructionist perspective.

MIDDLE MANAGEMENT DEFINED

Middle management, as the category which bridges the upper and lower levels in the organization and implements the strategies developed at the top, is in general described in terms of its managerial roles: interpersonal, informational and decisional. These roles are relatively standardly described in terms of control, implementation, co-ordination, planning, problemsolving, communication, decision-making, etc. Although in practice it is almost impossible to indicate what kind of roles a middle manager is playing, these concepts serve as a yardstick for describing activities.

Middle management as a function in an organization is always 'in between'. In between the top of the organization and the work-force at the bottom. These 'in between' layers of middle managers have the task of turning the objectives of the organizations into concrete goals, targets and actions, transmitting information to lower or higher organization levels and picking up weak signals and translating them into significant information – significant in the sense that distinctions are created which can lead to discussion on possible steps to be taken and their likely consequences.

Middle management is not a well-defined concept: a chain of middle-line managers with formal authority, which connects the operating core to the strategic apex (Mintzberg, 1975) or a chain which runs from just below the top to the first-line supervisors. The middle managers in this chain differ in status, knowledge, career possibilities, responsibilities, etc. The only thing they have in common is that they all are *in between*, not an easy place in any organization. All textbooks on management and organization refer to this difficult position.

Although many roles are discerned in relation to middle management (Mintzberg, 1973), as far as change is concerned the communicative role (interpersonal, informational and decisional) is the most important, but at the same time is the most neglected. The modernist tradition in the science of Management and Organization is primarily based, as Gergen (1992) notes, on the Enlightenment presumption of the world as 'one great machine', on the 'human organism as a simple programmable machine' (Kilduff, 1993: 17) and with the neglect therefore of the social relations and interactions of the workplace (Rabinbach, 1990).

In general the scientific description of middle management puts an emphasis on the necessity of a calculating attitude. For instance, middle management has to motivate its 'subordinates' in such a way that their behaviour leads to better benefits for the organization, or there is an emphasis on a linear causality on, for instance, task characteristics and psychological characteristics, between pay and motivation to work.

MIDDLE MANAGEMENT AND COMMUNICATION

In traditional communication theory reference is almost always to the Shannon/Weaver model. In communication an input is transformed by encoding and decoding resulting in another meaning or output, which is fed back to the sender. Noise is mentioned when there are difficulties in the decoding or encoding. In this model noise is an interference with the reception of the intended message. As Treece (1994) states 'less than perfect communication occurs because of weakness on the part of the sender or the receiver of the message, or of both, and also because of influence exerted along the way'. With this description Treece treats communication as an input–output system in which successful communication is primarily affected by the minds of the sender or receiver. Communication is considered effective if the idea formed by the receiver is similar to the one originally formulated by the sender.

The Shannon/Weaver model is based on the following suppositions: first, language enters the picture as a system for expressing conceptual formations. Thought exists independently of language, but there is the belief that 'in the possibility of full and perfect embodiment of thought in language and the structures of repetition that guarantee it' (Connor, 1989: 139), or as Whorf states: 'Talking, or the use of language, is supposed only to 'express' what is essentially already formulated nonlinguistically' (Whorf, in Mattheissen, 1993: 195). This 'mind-based' model is considered the common-sense model of language and thought. A model in which meaning originates within the individual mind. The basic assumption here is that our language about the world operates as a mirror of the world which presupposes a belief in a knowable world, in universal properties and truth through method (Gergen, 1992, 1994).

Second, if in communication theory the interpersonal metafunction is interpreted as verbal action then interpersonal meaning is from that point of view not enacted but primarily represented. Language as verbal action enters into the picture as a system for expressing conceptual formations. This is what Sampson (1989) calls the North American ideal of 'self-contained individualism', which sees the manager primarily as a 'problem solver', as a cognitive universe, a dynamic centre of awareness, judgement and action.

Communication is considered to be a linear input–output process and the individual to be a container of mental processes and structures, expressed by language. Information, therefore, is primarily concerned with 'information located in the individual's mind . . . . Language enters into the picture as a system for expressing conceptual formations' (Matthiessen, 1993: 194). Managers are analysers of data who solve problems that are represented to them (Boland, et al., 1994).

Third, there is a difference between communication and meaning. Communication in the Shannon/Weaver model is restricted to symbolic interaction and representation. Meaning-making includes the individual's interpretation of and reasoning about the world. Interpersonal meaning is enacted instead of being represented. Meaning-making involves an ongoing exchange and negotiation of meaning through which humans are enacted as interacting persons. Language processing is primarily a collaborative effort towards intersubjective validation of 'knowledge, and therefore also a product of social collaboration', and cannot be considered from an 'inter-organism-nor from a representation point of view' (Matthiessen, 1993: 196, 223). Meaning, therefore, as an ongoing process within the human relationship and in which meanings are continuously reconstituted as words continuously defer to other words (Gergen, 1994). Rationality is generated in processes of social interaction and truth therefore is 'the product of the collectivity of truth makers' (Gergen, 1982; 207). This implies that meaning reaches representation through the players (expression) and the context of meaning creation is a continuously shifting one.

As Gadamer states:

> When we enter into a dialogue with another person and then are carried along further by the dialogue, it is no longer the will of the individual person . . . that is determinative. Rather the law of the subject matter is at issue in the dialogue and elicits statements and counter-statements and in the end plays them in each other.
>
> (Gadamer, 1965:)

This is clearly different from the traditional conception of the mind-based model that emphasizes that there are barriers in communication due to filtering, manipulation of information, selective perception, emotion and language used. It is also the model based on the illusion of the rational and reflective agent-subject who is capable of acting autonomously. A model that Matthiessen (1993: 194) labels as 'the folk-model of the individual's mind'.

To talk about barriers in communication implies that communication can be rationalized so that everyone understands perfectly what is brought forward. It is the ideal of perfect communication, of language as a carrier of meanings, but this is an ideal which does not exist, as languaging takes place in a discursive context. Meanings are created in languaging and understanding is a form of giving meaning to an experience. Yet in this process of languaging meanings are at the same time reconstituted. Meanings not only refer to other words but are also context dependent. Shifts in meaning implies a shifting of contexts, and shifts in contexts can change meanings.

Therefore communication is both structure and process, content and expression, and knowledge nothing more than a process of intersubjective validation (Matthiessen, 1993).

Fourth in the language of organizations many new words are invented, for instance empowerment, re-engineering, core competencies, team management etc. Often words are added to the single word 'management', as for instance participative management, management by objectives, management by exception, etc. which indicates that something is not there, but should get attention.

The use of these concepts suggests that there is 'an essential reality – an origin to which they refer' (Derrida, 1978; Lemke, 1994; Sampson, 1989). The use, for instance, of a concept like empowerment suggests there is either the presence of empowerment, or the absence in terms of non-empowerment, there is either resistance or absence of resistance. It is what Matthiessen (1993) labels as 'folk model': the reification of experience where processes are construed as things.

In the language of everyday common sense *A attracts B so B moves* – a complex of two clauses; in the language of science, *attraction causes movement, attraction is the cause of movement*, and so on – where the every day clause complex, the sequence of two processes of action, has been 'compressed' into one clause with nominalized elements, a single process of being. ... When they are reconstrued as

46

things, processes lose their location in time and also their participants; for instance *A attracts B* is very likely to be reconstrued simply as *attraction*.

(Matthiessen, 1993: 193)

It is this change in the grammar, as Matthiessen observes, that definitely entailed a change in world-view, towards a static, reified world. This reification is exemplified in the common concepts used in speaking and writing about organizations in which concepts are used in an absolute and static way, and as having a significance in itself. Empowerment, team management, participative management, quality, flexibility, etc. are relational concepts defined by what is not empowerment, not participative, etc. They are relational 'as they are organized around a structure of presence and absence' (Kilduff, 1993: 17).

Relational concepts are based on what is and what is not. The balancing of these two is a dynamic and often a violent process (Cooper, 1989). One can not have both and the tendency is often to maximize one of the two opposites. Between novelty (change) and confirmation (structure) is a certain tension. Too much novelty makes people mad, too much confirmation can lead to a *status quo* and therefore the decline and death of the system. There is always a violent hierarchy between opposites, in which the one wants to turn over, to dominate the other, and vice versa (Cooper, 1989). Balancing opposites is a dynamic process.

MIDDLE MANAGEMENT FROM A SOCIAL CONSTRUCTIONIST PERSPECTIVE

As stated before, in communication language is neither representational nor the expression of inner mental states (Shotter, 1993). Meanings are constructed in the course of action and are therefore always multiple and ambiguous. Shotter (1989, 1993: 148) differentiates between the manager as a 'scientist' and the manager as a 'practical author'. He raises the question 'what is it that makes a manager a good manager?' A question immediately followed by the remark that such a question has nothing to do with 'finding and applying a true or false theory, but something with a complex of issues centred on the provision of an *intelligible formulation* of what has become, for the others in the organization, a chaotic welter of impressions'.

47

... Good managers when faced with such unchosen conditions, can, by producing an appropriate *formulation* of them,
create (a) a 'landscape' of enabling constraints relevant for
a range of next possible actions; (b) a network of 'moral
positions' or 'commitments' (understood in terms of the
rights and duties of the 'players' on that landscape); and
(c) are able to argue persuasively and authoritatively for
this 'landscape' among those who must work within it.

(Shotter, 1993: 148)

This careful description of 'good managers' captures relevant
points in the discussion on management and leadership. It
captures the tension of 'enabling constraints' and what it requires
from a manager. Also the tension between duties and rights of
the 'players' and focusses the attention on the importance of the
communication process and the process of creating meaning. The
term 'landscape' opens up possibilities, without at the same time
stating what should be seen and how that landscape should be
described. This process of communication must be justified or
justifiable, as well as 'grounded' or 'rooted' in some way in
circumstances others share (Shotter, 1993).

With this statement Shotter argues that the image of the
manager as a scientist or realist raises difficulties. The manager's
skill lies not primarily in problem-solving, but in problem-
setting. Problem-setting is creating a context for raising questions, for exchanging views, for making distinctions and
therefore for creating new meanings. Problem-setting is an invi-
tation to experiment and to learn by allowing that 'what not' is
allowed to enter into the dialogue.

Human interaction is communication and communication
builds upon previous communication and reproduces itself.
Contrary to the classic Shannon-Weaver model, it is the understanding of the receiver which is constitutive for communication
which implies that the sender cannot be the point of departure
for the analysis of communication patterns (see also In't Veld et
al., 1991). Distinctions that remain undrawn are not (Bateson,
1979), which implies that where no distinctions are made no
form of communication will take place.

Organizations are networks of conversation and those who
participate in these networks are involved in the processes of
creating and maintaining meanings. Change can only take place

when these networks of conversations change in the meanings given to experiences. It does not make much sense to change one individual if at the same time the question is not raised as to what this implies for the different networks and how these networks will deal with these changes. Even the power given to a person to force changes will lead in due time to the undoing of that power, as the network will structure itself in such a way that the conditions for the undoing of not accepted power will be created.

Networks of conversation are the contexts which surround the individual, the continuously shifting and developing discursive space. In this space there is the continuous interpenetration, the interplay of subject and object (the both/and) in which neither has full primacy.

The field of organization science has developed rapidly during the last thirty years and has become 'booming business' not only in relation to books and journals in this field, but also in relation to management development, training and consultancy. The concept of organization change has become an important item on the agenda of many organizations. In this attractive market is it necessary to capture the attention of those who carry managerial responsibilities.

The following quote from a 1994 brochure of one of the leading international consulting firms is an interesting way of drawing the attention of top and high-level managers. Interesting because it reflects to its potential clients that the consultancy firm understands the needs and worries of top managers and at the same time suggests that the consultancy firm can, on the basis of this understanding, support the manager in his lonely fight:

> Building a work-force in which employees are enabled and empowered to do their best takes time, commitment and often significant and continuous change. Change rarely comes without resistance. People are skeptical as to whether it will produce positive results and are concerned about its affect on them. They often look out for their own well being before that of the organization. To break down barriers to change and encourage people to work toward common objectives requires understanding, communication and a carefully managed change process. Once you understand your people's fears . . . .

In this quote all the stereotypes in relation to organization change are mentioned.

The quote makes manifest that each concept (fear, resistance, well-being, etc.) refers to its opposite, and is already mediated by the absent trace (Sampson, 1989). It is the suggestion that one has the choice between either/or – going on in the same difficult way or to have the courage to fight for a committed work-force which will lead to more positive results. At the same time the suggestive appeal is that there are tools and models available for solving the manager's problem with organization change and especially with the people involved. There are answers to people's resistance to change, their ego-orientedness and fears.

This common-sense model projects meaning and intentions into the action of others and 'it is to this projected meanings of certain actions and not to behavior itself that one reacts' (Gergen, 1982: 221). From that point of view our language of organizations is the language of our culture.

Organizations, as stated before, are networks of conversations, with their conversational realities (Shotter, 1993). In relation to change middle management plays a vital role. Change implies the creation of new meanings to situations, cognitions, and experiences. The necessity of change can only be expressed in language: language as a meaning-making system; language as content and expression, and in which content is realized through expression (Matthiessen, 1993).

The dominant notions in organization theory on communication, understanding and the creation of meaning are more complex than our dualistic models suggest and rest on a common-sense model, a folk model of language and thought. This model makes it possible to deny the communicative role of middle management. It is a model in which middle management merely represents the ideas of those in command or the ideas of those they supervise. This passive role is not true in reality. However, by denying the difficulties of the role of middle management the discussion on the difficulties of change will remain high on the organization agenda, instead of change as a natural phenomenon in which middle management plays such a fundamental role. The present interest on social constructivism, on language as a meaning system can contribute to a better understanding of this role.

REFERENCES

Bateson, G. (1979) *Mind and Nature*, London: Wildwood House.
Berger, P. and Luckmann T. (1966) *Social Construction of Reality*, Garden City, NY: Doubleday.
Bernstein, R.J. (1983) *Beyond Objectivism and Relativism; Science, Hermeneutics and Praxis*, Philadelphia: University of Philadelphia.
Boland, R.J., Tenkasi, R.V. and Te'eni, D. (1994) 'Designing information technology to support distributed cognition', *Organization Science* 5 (3): 456–76.
Boxer, P. and Kenny, V. (1990) 'The economy of discourses: a third order cybernatics?', *Human Systems Management*, 9.
Burrel, G. and Morgan, G. (1979) *Sociological Paradigms and Organizational Analysis*, London: Heinemann.
Connor, S. (1989) *Postmodernist Culture. An Introduction to Theories of the Contemporary*, Oxford: Basil Blackwell.
Cooper, R. (1989) 'Modernism, post modernism and organizational analysis 3: the contribution of Jacques Derrida', *Organizational Analysis* 10 (4).
Cooper, R. and Burrell, G. (1988) 'Modernism, post modernism and organizational analysis: an introduction', *Organizational Studies* 10 (4).
Deetz, S. (1994) 'The new politics in the workplace: ideology and other unobtrusive controls', in H.W. Simons and M. Billig (eds) *After Postmodernism. Reconstructing Ideology Critique*, London: Sage.
Derrida, J. (1978) *Writing and Difference*, Chicago: University of Chicago Press.
Gadamer, H.G. (1965) *Truth and Method*, translated and edited by G. Barden and J. Cumming, New York: Seabury Press.
Geertz, C. (1973) *The Interpretation of Culture*, New York: Basic Books.
Gergen, K.J. (1982) *Toward Transformation in Social Knowledge*, London: Sage.
— (1989) 'Warranting voice and the elaboration of the self', in J. Shotter and K.J. Gergen (eds), *Texts of Identity*, London: Sage.
— (1992) 'Organization theory in the postmodern era', in M. Reed and M. Hughes (eds) *Rethinking Organization*, London: Sage.
— (1994) *Realities and Relationships*, Cambridge: Harvard University Press.
Glaserfeld, E. von (1981) 'The concepts of adaptation and viability in a radical constructivist theory of knowledge', in J.E. Siegel, D.M. Brodzinsky and R.M. Golinkoff (eds) *New Directions in Piagetian Theory and Practice*, Philadelphia: Erlbaum.
— (1984) 'An introduction to radical constructivism', in P. Watzlawick (ed.), *The Invented Reality. How Do We Know What We Believe to Know? Contributions to Constructivism*, New York: Norton.
— (1987) *The Construction of Knowledge*, Seaside, CA: Intersystems.
In 't Veld, R., Schaap L., Termeer C.J.A.M. and Van Twist, M.J.W. (1991) *Autopoieses and Configuration Theory: New Approaches to Societal Steering*, Dordrecht: Kluwer.

Kilduff, M. (1993) 'Deconstructing organizations', *Academy of Management Review* **18** (1): 13–32.

Lemke, J.L. (1994) 'Discourse, dynamics, and social change', *Cultural Dynamics* **6** (1).

Matthiessen, C. (1993) 'The object of study in cognitive science in relation to its construal and enactment in language', *Cultural Dynamics* **6** (1–2): 187–243.

Maturana, H.R. and Varela, F.J. (1987) *The Tree of Knowledge. The Biological Roots of Human Understanding*, London: New Science Library.

Midler, C. (1993) *L'Auto qui n'existait pas. Management des Projets et Transformation de l'Entreprise*, Paris: InterEditions.

Mintzberg,H. (1973) *The Nature of Managerial Works*, New York: Harper and Row.

— (1975)'The manager's job: folklore and fact', *Harvard Business Review*, July–August.

Orlikowski, W.J. and Yates, W.J. (1995) 'Genre repertoire: the structuring of communicative practices in organizations', *Administrative Science Quarterly*, **39**.

Pinxten, R. and Farber, C.K. (1990) 'On learning a comparative view', *Cultural Dynamics* **III** (3): 233–52.

Rabinbach, A. (1990) *The Human Motor. Energy, Fatigue, and the Origins of Modernity*, New York: Basic Books.

Sampson, E.E. (1989) 'The deconstruction of the self', in J. Shotter and K.J. Gergen (eds), *Texts of Identity*, London: Sage.

Shannon, C. and W. Weaver (1949) *The Mathematical Theory of Communication*, Urbana: University of Illinois Press.

Shotter, J. (1989) 'Social accountability and social construction of "you"', in J. Shotter and K.J. Gergen (eds), *Texts of Identity*, London: Sage.

— (1993) *Conversational Realities. Constructing Life through Language*, London: Sage.

Treece, M. (1994) *Successful communication for business and the professions*, New York: Prentice Hall.

4

TRENDS IN EUROPEAN MIDDLE MANAGEMENT
Evidence from five countries[1, 2]

Fotis Vouzas, John G. Burgoyne and
Yves-Frédéric Livian

THE RESEARCH APPROACH

The research reported here is empirical in the sense that it describes information and views collected from members of fifteen organizations from five European countries in relation to questions formed from an examination of the literature relating to the changing nature of middle managers (MMs) (as reported in chapter 1), and then seeks to draw conclusions in relation to these questions.

This methodology section of the chapter sets out the philosophical (ontological/epistemological assumptions) underlying its approach, discusses some of the features of the study that will help the reader make an assessment on the veracity and generalizability of the conclusion, supported by some description of the data collection and analysis approach.

The study works from the assumption that the managerial and organizational world are socially constructed, in terms of the tradition of thinking initiated by Berger and Luckman (1966), Silverman (1970) and others. However, it does not go to the extreme view that language has no referential content at all, that language is a set of terms that only have meaning in each other's contexts, a view related to post-structuralist linguistics often associated in its origin with the work of Saussure (see Culler, 1976). The outworking of this position is to render theory-building an entirely rhetorical and discursive activity that makes theory and theory-building an esoteric activity that is increasingly inaccessible and meaningless to the citizens of organizations and practitioners of management (Ackroyd, 1992).

The framework of this study is that management theory is itself one or more sets of social constructions, as is the realm of organization and management practice. The former is at least in part 'about' the latter, and the process of this study has been to collect evidence on the changing construction of MMs in organizational worlds, with questions drawn from the theory, and to draw some conclusions about these theoretical questions. Although this study is not based on the positivist assumptions of stable relationships between concrete events in a world external to theory which can be described in that theory and generalized across temporal, spatial and cultural domains, there is a representational claim concerning one domain of social construction of another, which makes veracity and generalizability discussable.

The claims to veracity in this study rely partly, as they must in most qualitative empirical work, on the skill and 'good faith' of the researchers in understanding and portraying the constructions of the study sites in a way which is both true to the site and communicates this outside it. Certain features were included in the data collection and analysis with the aim of increasing confidence in veracity, without of course guaranteeing it, and within the practical and logistical constraints of the study:

1 Multiple informants (stakeholders – Burgoyne, 1994) were interviewed in each research site, typically one or more senior managers, a small sample (3–5) of MMs as identified in the terms of the field of study in the light of the formal definitions of the concept, a senior personnel/human resource manager, the most specific person with a role related to any 'quality management' processes or initiatives.
2 Each site was written up as an integrated case study, with the focus on drawing out the commonalities of meaning and understanding in each site. Where possible these accounts were checked back with representatives of the field sites.
3 In the analytical stage all three authors separately, then together, examined and interpreted the data in relation to the research questions to reach at least intersubjectively acceptable conclusions.

On generalizability, the logic of this chapter is to draw conclusions from the sample, and discuss the extent to which various propositions concerning MM are true of them. Claims to generalizability are left open, the chapter attempts to be as clear as possible about the features of the research that might justify a degree of confidence in generalizing the conclusions.

The study draws conclusions from data from fifteen organizations from five countries (Greece, France, Portugal, The Netherlands, the UK). The three organizations in each country were two private sector engineering or chemical sector manufacturers and one health sector hospital. The logic was to achieve spread and comparability, and some opportunity to consider private and public sector practice. Small firms were ruled out so that sites would be large enough to have a 'middle' according to most of the definitions of MM.

In choosing companies for the sample, the principle was to accept companies that were judged as normal, ordinary, representative by those helping to identify and obtain access to the sample. Organizations that were thought to be exceptional, or unusual, including being known for implementing 'new' management ideas, were omitted. The sample was subjectively chosen to represent the norm of corporate practice in the country concerned.

The hospital sample was chosen by selecting a general hospital serving a large town or city. Contextual data on the hospitals suggest that they tend to be subject to organizational formulae and infrastructural features that are relatively standardized within nation-state boundaries, which gives a kind of ground for confidence in generalization from this small number of organizations. The partial exception to this was the French hospital, which was a military hospital accepting civilian patients. The exception is only partial because this is itself not an uncommon practice in France. This case does have some features related to a military command structure and being in the sphere of influence of a Defence Ministry, which would be representative of several but not all hospitals serving the French public.

Inferences about generalizability can also be made from the data itself. To the extent to which sites themselves attribute changes in MMs to social, economic, political, cultural and infrastructural features, and similar examples arise across the sample, confidence in generalizability may be increased. To the extent to which changes relate to seemingly voluntarist internal choices of organizational design, then the reverse would be true.

Generalizing over time is likely to be particularly problematic in this, as in any, study of change. The focus of the study is on change in progress in 1994. Some results may be era-specific. For example reducing MM numbers may be less apparent in this era because it has happened, where it is going to happen, already. Broader generalizations can only be attributed in terms of larger patterns.

The results reported are about rates of change, not the 'absolute' levels of the things that are changing. Absence of change may be because a feature already exists. For example, in some parts of the health sector commitment is not found to be increasing because it has always been relatively high.

Finally, the generalizability of conclusions depends partly on the question to which the conclusion is addressed. The principle of refutation (Popper, 1963) from positivism can arguably carry over to this kind of study. If a research question is itself about the truth of a generalization (for example in this context, that a homogeneous new entity, the Euro-MM, is emerging to standardize national difference) then a small sample that shows exception to this is sufficient to refute the generalization (that is, significant diversity of MM practice between nations in a sample of fifteen organizations is sufficient to show that the Euro-middle manager is not a strong universal current reality).

The practicalities of the research as a series of steps, having a bearing on the interpretation of the veracity and generalizability of the conclusions have been:

1 The formulation of questions about MM and its context.
2 Choosing and accessing fifteen organizations from five countries, with a degree of standardization of the sectors represented, and using informed subjective opinion to select normal, and reject exceptional, organizations.
3 Collection of information from multiple stakeholders/informants within the managerial domain. It is important to note that the study takes data from the managerialist construction of MM reality to the realm of management theory, of which it is one of the objects. This is not to deny, as is important from a critical theory perspective (Alvesson and Willmott, 1992), that the whole object of management theory may or must be wider than managerialism itself.
4 Initially portraying the fifteen organizations as integral cases drawing together the picture from the multiple informants.

5 Achieving intersubjective agreement on the interpretation of the cases in terms of the research questions concerning change in MM.

As in all such research the processes of question-seeking, data-seeking, sense-making and conclusion-drawing represent an endless series of choices and rejected alternatives. In the data-reduction process of rendering a chapter-length account of this process only a few of these choices regarded as key can be accounted for with any degree of adequacy. For the rest, the best that can be achieved by way of evidence to give confidence in veracity and generalizability is to declare that the researchers were guided in making the myriad choices by principles of authenticity to the data and open-mindedness a priori on the answers to the research questions posed, and as a research team challenged and monitored each other on the application of these principles.

THE RESEARCH RESULTS

The research results are initially presented as descriptive observations of what was found under each of the fifteen change headings, across the fifteen organizations, pointing out some of the special cases and differences. This is followed by a table in which, while acknowledging that this is based on qualitative data, each of the fifteen organizations are judged on each of the fifteen change characteristics. Conclusions are then drawn in terms of the extent to which each of the change characteristics is found to be enacted and constructed in the organizations studied. National and sector differences are also discussed. Prior to the presentation of these results the operationalizability of the MM concept is considered.

In all cases it was possible, in discussion with organizational members, to identify people/roles that fitted the broad operational definition of MMs adopted in this study: the wide hierarchy band between undirected strategy formers and basic work supervisors, involved in work that is middle range in terms of scope and impact. All organizations studied had identifiable elements of hierarchy, though varyingly configured in functional divisions, formal command chains, forms of matrix organization and elements of temporary project group structuring. Although many of the organizations studied had experienced 'delayering' and becoming leaner, this generally could be accounted for as making smaller existing pyramidal forms rather than any more radical form of organization. However various project, matrix and cost centre adaptations to the hierarchy were in evidence, giving the hierarchical forms a more flexible and temporary nature. A significant conclusion to be drawn from this rather basic observation is that the concept of MM is sufficiently stable to survive the current forms of change in these 'ordinary' organizations.

Although MM so defined, as a generic term, was acceptable as making sense in the field settings, it was not necessarily or often a term that was used as a formal or everyday term in day-to-day organizational discourses. Organizations had their own specific terminologies for jobs and grades. These varied in whether they used the term 'management' at all, and there were some situations where the term 'senior management' was used to differentiate the status of some managers who fitted our broad definition from others who fitted it from positions closer to supervision. It was possible to identify roles in the hospital setting that fitted the MM definition, where these were either in the middle of functional hierarchies (for example administration, nursing) or in more integrated structures (as in the UK and The Netherlands).

We now present the results taking the fifteen hypotheses which have been analysed in Chapter 1.

Qualitative observations on the change areas, dealt with in the order established in the literature review

Increased commitment (and the nature of the opposite, resistance, alienation)

Changing attitude to authority demanding more participative style of management, the implementation of new management initiatives giving increased but bounded autonomy to MMs, restructuring creating jobs that were previously done by more people in larger organizations, and an increased awareness of the nature and situation of the 'businesses' (including public sector), are tending to increase the commitment of MM population, often because they feel part of organizations with increasing problems and challenges. There is some national variation in the form that this takes. The Portuguese organizations have a very strong organizational culture based on small production scale, family, traditional organizations where organizational difficulties trigger commitment in the form of behaviour based on strong loyalties. There are some similarities in the UK, but with the loyalty being to organizations as institutions which MMs feel committed to supporting as part of the fabric of society rather than to families, though one of the UK firms had reached this state through a paternalistic family ownership history.

It is important to be aware that the data is about rate of increase in commitment, not its absolute level. The majority of the hospital sites had maintained either relatively high or relatively low levels of commitment. The struggle for power between doctors and nurses and a 'don't care' mentality of the public sector employees is a very common factor that influences the commitment of the MMs in countries such as Greece, Portugal and France, and to a lesser extent in The Netherlands and the UK. In these latter sites higher commitment is maintained due to professional values and the personal values that attract people to work in the caring professions. In these situations MMs are drawn into greater commitment as they seek to influence involving, though often difficult, attempts at organizational reform that are going on. In other situations, particularly the Greek organizations, a degree of MM detachment was a consistent factor due to the very strict hierarchy and to the lack of a strong corporate identity, frustrations experienced in bringing about changes and the constraints of formal regulations.

Reduced security and conventional career progression

For those MMs who have been able to keep their jobs during restructuring, implementation of new initiatives, delayering, downsizing, etc. there is a sense of re-established security, and career aspirations have moderated in the context of the simpler structures surrounding them. This is the general picture in the UK, French and Dutch private sector, where career planning and development systems still operate. One of the French companies provides an exception as it faces restructuring and downsizing. At the other extreme the Greek and Portuguese health organizations currently maintain 'jobs for life' arrangements which are sufficiently believed in to give a strong sense of security. Greek and Portuguese managers, both public and private sector, feel secure because of the relative rigidities of their organizations, and the forms of job protection built into their formal and cultural arrangements.

Reduction/change due to information technology

In contrast to the dramatic views of some consultants and organizational theory specialists concerning the effect of information technology (IT), the vast majority of the MMs, and those around them, in almost all organizations studied mentioned no current major effect of the introduction of IT on their work in both sectors. While some companies have undergone restructurings that have brought in new production, work and information systems involving significant IT, and reduced numbers of MMs, the conclusion is that for the remaining MMs the nature of their work, or the likelihood of its continuing existence, is not currently changing dramatically because of IT. More modest and incremental effects were reported in some cases, along the lines of IT helping with the efficiency of some routine operations freeing effort for other things. Almost all MMs were familiar and used computer facilities in their daily work, and dealt with corporate information systems through them. There are no major national or sector differences in the examination of this variable concerned with MM change.

This evidence in no way suggests that IT has not or is not having dramatic effects on how organizations work or their efficiency, what it does suggest is that the basic human work of translating between strategy and operations, working in the middle of a human command hierarchy, introducing new working arrangements and getting people to work together is not becoming dramatically different as IT permeates organizations. It may be that it is clerical support to MM that has been substituted by IT, and many of those gains and changes are now history.

Incorporation of previously separate functions

There was little evidence of this as a transition in the organizations at the time of investigation or in their recent history. For those organizations that had been through rationalization at an earlier time this transition may have been achieved in that era. However, the more general observation was that where in-house services had ceased to exist they were often omitted or bought in as an external service in cases of real necessity. A tendency towards more MM work in co-ordinating, liaising with and managing external contractors was noted in the leaner firms innovating in products and production processes.

Less tightly specified role, more self-determination

Generally MMs were found to have quite tightly specified roles. Many of these are framed in job descriptions and organizational processes, which do not enable them to be more flexible or more self-determined, and even where organizations appear more informal or organic MMs are surrounded by a dense network of expectations and obligations that have the same effect.

Most of the organizations were engaged in change activities associated with quality initiatives, and these were affecting role specificity. In the majority of cases, particularly in the private sector, where the main approach was standards/certification based (pursuit and operation of ISO and related accreditation) an increase in formalized procedures, many of them impacting MM work, was the consequence. In the case of UK and Dutch firms where some loosening of MM roles was found, this was closely associated with a move to more processual and less bureaucratic approaches to quality management. A lessening of role specificity was also found in the French and Portuguese hospital organizations, and in these cases it took the form of a climb-down from a very high level of centrally run rule and regulation controlled work.

In the health sector in general MMs have a very tight, specialized role compared with their colleagues in the industry sector. In the public hospitals, especially in countries like Greece and Portugal, hierarchy, discipline and formal relationships are very important. Roles are defined by the Ministry of Health and imposed through regulations and decrees. In The Netherlands and France there is a move towards a more autonomous and flexible role for the nurse. In France 'Projet D' Etablissement' has given chief and supervisory nurses more responsibilities, flexibility and autonomy. In Holland on the other hand, restructuring and the introduction of new management initiatives has exposed MMs more to local pressures and demands.

In the UK, even though there has been a major change in the health system with the introduction of directorates and the elimination of the functional organization, this has been achieved through redefined, and in some cases new, MM roles that have been specified with some care and constrained to avoid disturbing other power interests, while at the same time being the location of demands for business performance.

Quantitative reduction

There is little evidence of a current reduction or delayering of the MM population in the sample, though some have been through this in the more distant past in the private sector. In the health sector there are few signs of reducing numbers of MMs within hospital organizations. Exceptions are Holland where there was speculation that in future years the hospital will need less managers, and France where one company was likely to engage in staff reduction generally. Where further staff reductions were possible it was not thought likely or feasible that MMs would take a disproportionate share of this. MMs in the health sector have less chances of being laid off, since in Greece, Portugal and probably France staff have 'life-time employment'.

Less supervisory responsibility due to increased autonomy and self-direction of work groups

In the majority of the organizations, teams, in the sense of self-directed work groups, are not formally in operation and tend to be temporary, and not to cover the whole organization when they do occur. Most organizations did have an emphasis on group working, but in a form that was supervised, and led by MMs.

One UK organization was closer to this process with formally operating teams and the whole organization operating under several continuous improvement teams covering all levels and functions of the organization. In this situation MMs did not have any supervisory responsibility, and occupied varying membership and co-ordinating roles in teams. In this situation MMs survive as a pool of managerial labour still contributing to the alignment of strategy and operations through their membership of task and project groups. In a less formal way MMs in one of the Dutch organizations had significantly devolved supervision by delegation, in the context of an organizational restructuring based on the principle of involving MMs more in strategy.

It appears from this limited amount of data that this change in the nature of MMs only occurs in the context of a significant new structure and organizational design philosophy. It does not appear to be a change that takes place as a consequence of a change of individual MM style. However it was reported that MMs with longer histories of having operated with a more direct style of managing had greater difficulty in adapting to this different way of operating.

These observations apply in the health sector. Even though some hospitals had introduced a more decentralized and flexible system of management, teams were not central to this change and MMs identified themselves as directing and managing. The French and Dutch hospitals were considering more team orientation and consequent reduction in the supervisory role for MMs, but this was unrealized at the time of the study.

In Greece and Portugal a traditional directive style of management (and being managed) was seen as being part of the culture. A managing director of a Portuguese company said that 'Portuguese are not Japanese'. Similarly in French organizations in both sectors quality circles were reported as having been tried and failed, this being attributed in part to a resistance to style change by MMs. Team-working was under discussion in the Dutch organizations, but top managements were sceptical.

New contract relationship

In general there was a demand from the top management for flexibility from the MMs, but not for creativity or innovation. Creativity and innovation were still seen as the responsibilities of the R&D departments or specialists or consultants. MMs saw themselves, and were seen as, more the guardians of well-known territories and the implementers of planned changes and less as participants in the creative and innovative processes.

Organizations with initiatives towards TQM and process re-engineering emphasized the need for flexibility and creativity, but only in the domain of implementing new systems. With these new production and work arrangements there is also a move towards standardization, which is not compatible with flexibility and creativity.

New set of roles – teacher, coach, facilitator, etc.

Very few of these roles were being practised by MMs. It was more common for an MM to be a teacher or a trainer for new employee or first line supervisors, than a coach, a facilitator, etc. of existing staff. There were some MMs who did not want to practise these roles, because they felt they would lose their power, have less chances for promotion, become isolated from top management and move towards the shop-floor people.

There were cases where MMs acted as coaches and facilitators in an informal way because the size of the company, the nature of the industry, the personality of the manager and sometimes the manager's age (young managers were more willing to be coaches and facilitators than old managers) allowed this. These practices occurred particularly in one Portuguese and one UK firm, but in both cases as a matter of long-standing tradition – the former of company loyalty, the latter of professional allegiance. These behaviours and practices were, however, part of a pattern of stability rather than of change. Some examples of facilitating behaviour were found within the implementation of the less proceduralized forms of TQM, but these were by supervisors, for whom it was an expansion and enrichment of role, rather than by MMs. In the health sector team-working was universally part of the nursing culture, within which facilitative leadership was only acceptable in relation to trainee nurses, not qualified ones.

The emergence of these 'new roles' was also found to be difficult or not achievable in the culture of Greek and Portuguese MMs, due to the strict hierarchical lines, and the organizational cultures defining them. In the French organizations the possibility of this approach to management was recognized, but there was scepticism about it, and the tradition of the MM cadres as differentiated groups appeared to make the possibility of this boundary-eroding behaviour difficult to consider as a realistic possibility. In the cases of UK and Dutch companies there were attempts to persuade and train managers to adopt these roles.

A hypothesis that emerges from these observations is that a change in this aspect of MM behaviour may be difficult, or even not feasible, in national cultures that rely on the maintenance of power–distance relationships (Hofstede, 1980).

Involvement in strategy

Basically, in all sectors and countries MMs are not directly involved in the strategic decision-making process. They usually make suggestions, submit proposals to top management, attend some meetings related to strategy design, or develop an annual or biannual business plan that has to fit into the overall organizational strategy. Top management demand that they think strategically and less operationally, but what they mean by this is that MMs should understand the strategy better so that they can 'own' it and implement it more intelligently without detailed direction. In some cases MMs influence the formation and implementation of strategy and sometimes they participate in the formation and early development stage of strategic decisions, but they are less a party to the final act of commitment.

Middle managers frequently expressed resentment at being excluded from strategy formation and choice, feeling that they could contribute because of their skills and experience. In some cases top management did not trust MMs to participate in strategy, and in some other cases MMs were not willing to participate, considering involvement in strategy as an extra burden outside their responsibilities. In the private sector (engineering companies), MMs had more chances for involvement and influence on strategic aspects than in public sector, partly because in the latter case strategy is significantly a matter of interpreting government policy rather than setting plans in the light of operating experience.

In countries were organization is seen as being strongly formally hierarchical, with a concentration of the power at the top as in, Greece, Portugal and to a lesser degree France, MMs are reluctant to participate and top management is automatically in charge of strategy. On the other hand in the UK and Holland, with the introduction of participative styles of management and in conjunction with the implementation of quality initiatives, MMs were found to have more strategic influence. However, these are matters of degree and, generally speaking, there were more similarities than differences in comparing MM involvement in strategy in the countries of the sample.

Development of new attitudes and competencies: people-oriented skills

The majority of MMs were found to have moved into this particular level of hierarchy either by promotion due to years of experience and technical expertise, or by education and formal qualification for the specific positions. They usually had excellent technical skills and knowledge but they lacked managerial skills and knowledge. Managerial, people-oriented skills became a necessity to MMs due to the flow of new 'knowledge workers', introduction of sophisticated systems in production and work flow areas, and increasing demands for managers to develop teams, business plans, handle conflicts, organize meetings, etc. Human resource management practices, and quality initiatives (which typically involve MM training/briefing elements) play an important role in helping MMs to develop these skills. In most cases, MMs are getting general management knowledge through sporadic seminars organized by outside consultants. The emphasis has been more on the technical side than the people side of management in most of the cases in this study.

In most of the companies there were no special programmes designed for MMs. Many MMs sought these skills and competencies by investing personally in external seminars or courses as part of their own personal, professional and career development. In some cases there were MMs who felt that there was no time for development of new skills.

Most of the MMs mentioned the following skills as increasingly necessary to perform their jobs:

- listening skills
- conflict handling
- organizing meetings
- time planning
- motivation skills
- team building

In the health sector the emphasis had historically been on the development of technical rather than managerial skills. Only recently had public hospitals started to develop educational and training programmes covering general management aspects. Middle managers in the hospitals did not feel the need for management of people skills. This was due to the emphasis on specialization and professionalization in this sector, but hospitals in Holland and the UK had moved towards having more people management oriented MM roles. For the health sector, in Greece the majority of MMs did not perceive a need for people-oriented skills, and there was no effort to develop those skills either by MMs for themselves or by the organization or by the Ministry of Health. In France and Portugal there were initiatives for the development of training programmes focusing on people management skills.

Key players in moving from 'old' to the 'new'

The MM population was found, in general, still to be playing a routine and operational role. Participation in strategy formation, as discussed, was at a very low level compared with implementation. Top management was found to hang on to the role of development of new initiatives using specialist functions and consultants if they needed help. There were several organizations in the sample where MMs played an important role in the introduction, support and maintenance of these initiatives through being their enthusiastic supporters. Young managers were found to be more willing to take part in new programmes and initiatives and risks of this sort.

In organizations that moved into restructuring and introduction of new initiatives, MMs had experienced periods of greater autonomy and had had chances to be 'role models', or 'agents of change'. In contrast, in more stable organizations MMs felt isolated, and spent their time in routine work.

There were no major differences by sector in this change area. Only in the hospital in Holland due to restructuring and in the military hospital in France due to the introduction and implementation of Project d' Etablissement, did MMs have an important role in representing new initiatives.

Business orientation

Even though very few writers mentioned this hypothesized change, in our sample there is a significant move in this direction in many of the organizations. Where there is less current change of this sort is in the private sector, because this emphasis was phased in earlier. Top management demand that MMs act more as managers and less as supervisors, fire-fighters or as inter-mediaries in communication channels. MMs are having more cost and profit responsibilities, they usually are responsible for setting a small-scale business plan, and are frequently evaluated based on the results. In some organizations they are very close to the customers and trying to establish strong relationships. This is due to the efforts of most of the companies in cost reduction increased efficiency and effectiveness, improvement in quality, etc. MMs had to prove, in the majority of the cases, that they could add value to the organization.

The introduction and implementation of quality programmes or initiatives have a major effect in this kind of change. Companies are forcing the measurement of almost every activity and the putting of a value to every action or process. Middle managers are both the subject of this process and involved in its application to basic work flows. In the health sector, MMs come from a less business-oriented background in almost all the hospitals. In The Netherlands, the UK and France policy and senior management is pushing in the direction of giving MMs a more business-oriented mission, and retaining and rewarding those that do so.

Shift in balance from professional to more managerial work

This area of change was found in its most pronounced form in the UK, Dutch and French health organizations where it is being brought about by varying forms of 'modernization'. Although the professional/managerial relationship in the health industry is usually thought of in terms of clinicians and administration/ management (Burgoyne and Lorbiecki, 1993) the bulk of MM activity involves those with a nursing professional background since this is the area with more people to manage, and which provides the bulk of patient contact and care.

In the private sector is has been more normal for MMs to be those who have moved on from technical/professional, for example engineering, to more managerial work. However, in more specialist-product organizations (UK C2, Portugal C2 and Greece C1) resistance was found to this shift due to loyalty to and the status of the professional/technical function, and perceptions of the labour market utility of remaining as up to date as a professional/technical expert.

Experience of increased pressure and stress

Increased pressure and stress was a dominant phenomenon for MMs in all organizations of the sample. There are several reasons:

- increased workload, more responsibilities (most of the times 'delegated' from top management
- the 'business orientation' trend
- alienation from top management
- government interventions and regulations
- conflict with colleagues and superiors in the context of multiple demands
- new initiative overload
- pressure to update skills and knowledge, sometimes with certification.

There are no major national differences, except for the public (health) sector in Greece and Portugal, where MMs enjoy a lifetime employment that reduces stress due to insecurity, but in these situations there are other frustrations and sources of stress, including conflict with doctors and tight state control.

Patterns in the observations

As a route to identifying patterns in this qualitative data, Tables 4.1–4.3 display summaries of our interpretation of whether or not each kind of change was current in each of the organizations (Table 4.1), and their frequency of occurrence overall and in sector groups (Table 4.2) and in national groups (Table 4.3). It needs to be emphasized, in line with the stance outlined in the 'research approach' section above, that these are qualitative interpretations of how MM change is constructed in the different sites that are codified and counted rather than 'objective' measures of concrete realities in terms of a number of variables.

Table 4.1 shows how each organization codified by sector and national group is assessed in terms of whether or not each of the kinds of change were current at the time of investigation (mid-1994). This mapping provides the intermediate level of analysis that is the basis of the further steps of data reduction in Tables 4.2 and 4.3 showing the frequencies of the changes overall and by sector (Table 4.2) and national groupings (Table 4.3). In all the tables the change areas are set out in the ordering established on the basis of the literature review reported in Chapter 1, from those where there was evidence of the change having occurred in organizational settings through to those that were wishes, predictions or normative prescriptions. Our results can be interpreted from one point of view as a further test of this ordering but also, and perhaps more meaningfully, as an indicator of which changes are under way at the time of this study, which are over, and which are mythological or, if they are to occur, are still in the future. Much of the research and literature reviewed previously in Chapter 1 is based on observations made in the 1980s and earlier. These summaries are the primary basis for the conclusions that we draw from this study.

CONCLUSIONS

The firmest overall conclusion that can be drawn is that MM is still subject to increasing pressure and stress, and experiencing the demand to develop new attitudes and competencies. On the basis of these organizations studies, the era of, possibly disproportional, decreases in the numbers of MMs is over, or not a process related to anything other than general organizational growth or contraction. Similarly the shift from technical and professional orientations to managerial and business orientations has taken place, except in the heath sector where it is a current issue.

The one area of change that is more real than it was judged to be historically is the increasing commitment to work and organizational priorities. The strong impression is that remaining MMs are being drawn into increasing patterns of hard work around central business processes in leaner, more simply structured organizations. Middle managers are involved in strategy implementation in the sense of a more immediate understanding of its current direction and their role in realizing it, and identifying issues pertinent to its continuous revision, as distinct from its pure formulation. There are some greater degrees of freedom from detailed structuring of MM work and roles, and scope for creativity and innovation, but only in the context of work tightly

Table 4.1 Occurrence of forms of MM change by organization

Change characteristic	UK			France			The Netherlands			Portugal			Greece		
	C1	C2	H	C1	C2	H	C1	C2	H	C1	C2	H	C1	C2	H
Increased pressure and stress	Y	Y	Y	Y	Y	Y	Y	Y	Y	Y	Y	Y	Y	Y	Y
Development of new attitudes and competences	Y	Y	Y	Y	Y	Y	Y	Y	Y	Y	N	N	Y	Y	Y
Reduction in numbers	N	N	N	Y	Y	Y	N	N	Y	N	N	N	N	N	N
Shift in balance from technical/professional to managerial work	N	N	Y	N	N	Y	N	N	Y	Y	N	N	N	N	N
Greater involvement in strategy	Y	N	N	N	N	N	Y	N	N	N	N	N	N	N	N
Change or reduction in role due to IT	N	N	Y	N	Y	N	N	Y	N	Y	N	N	N	N	N
Increased business orientation	Y	N	Y	N	N	Y	N	N	Y	N	N	N	N	N	N
New contract relationship: creativity, innovation	Y	N	N	Y	N	N	N	N	Y	N	N	N	N	N	N
Reduced security and career prospects	N	N	N	N	N	N	N	N	N	N	N	N	N	N	N
Incorporation of previously separate functions	N	N	N	N	N	N	N	N	N	N	N	N	N	N	N
Less supervision due to work team autonomy	Y	Y	N	Y	N	N	Y	N	N	N	N	Y	N	N	N
Less tightly specified role	Y	Y	N	N	N	N	Y	N	N	Y	Y	Y	N	N	N
Increased commitment	Y	Y	N	Y	Y	N	Y	Y	N	Y	Y	N	N	N	N
Key players in introducing new organizational forms	Y	N	N	N	N	N	Y	N	Y	N	N	N	N	N	N
New roles: coach, facilitator, teacher	Y	Y	N	Y	N	N	Y	N	N	N	N	N	N	N	N

C1 = Company 1, C2 = Company 2, H = Hospital. Y = yes, the characteristic was found. N = No, the characteristic was not found.

71

Table 4.2 Frequencies of change characteristics overall and by sector

Change characteristics in order of 'Facticity' as assessed from literature	Whole sample No. of orgs out of 15 with change	Private sector sample No of orgs out of 10 with change	Public/health sector sample No. of orgs out of 5 with change
Increased pressure and stress	15	10	5
Development of new attitudes and competences	13	9	4
Reduction in numbers	3	3	0
Shift in balance from technical/professional to managerial work	4	1	3
Greater involvement in strategy	3	3	0
Change or reduction in role due to IT	2	2	0
Increased business orientation	5	2	3
New contract relationship: creativity, innovation	4	3	1
Reduced security and career prospects	1	1	0
Incorporation of previously separate functions	0	0	0
Less supervision due to work team autonomy	3	3	0
Less tightly specified role	5	3	2
Increased commitment	8	7	1
Key players in introducing new organizational forms	4	3	1
New roles: coach, facilitator, teacher	4	4	0

Table 4.3 Frequency of change characteristics by country (no. out of three for each)

Change characteristics	UK	France	Netherlands	Portugal	Greece
Increased pressure and stress	3	3	3	3	3
Development of new attitudes and competences	3	3	3	1	3
Reduction in numbers	0	3	0	0	0
Shift in balance from technical/professional to managerial work	1	1	1	1	0
Greater involvement in strategy	1	0	1	1	0
Change or reduction in role due to IT	0	1	1	0	0
Increased business orientation	2	1	1	1	0
New contract relationship: creativity, innovation	1	1	2	0	0
Reduced security and career prospects	0	1	0	0	0
Incorporation of previously separate functions	0	0	0	0	0
Less supervision due to work team autonomy	2	0	1	0	0
Less tightly specified role	2	1	1	1	0
Increased commitment	2	1	2	3	0
Key players in introducing new organizational forms	1	0	2	1	0
New roles: coach, facilitator, teacher	2	1	1	0	0
TOTAL	20	17	19	12	6

focused on the operational achievement of shifting business targets. Middle managers are being required to achieve higher levels of performance against shifting business objectives from those that they manage, which is making new demands on MMs in terms of commitment to, and understanding of, business priorities, and to develop and exercise new skills of leadership and people management to deal with people from whom change and performance is being demanded, but for whom traditional forms of authoritative management continue to be less acceptable.

Comparing the private and public (health) sectors shows an overall similarity of pattern, with a few exceptions. As has been mentioned, a reorientation from technical/professional to managerial/business orientations is more current in the health sector, where MM work is changing but not reducing quantitatively as new forms of managerialism substitute for old forms of administration. With this change there is increased scope for entrepreneurialism and creativity, and some work that is less procedure and rule bound. Commitment is not escalating in quite the same way as in the private sector, due in part to the continuation of relatively high levels of organizational dedication and degrees of perceived stability associated with 'secure' state employment.

The data on national comparisons (Table 4.3) has to be interpreted with caution, but to the extent to which the small numbers of organizations are representative, as they were intended to be in their selection for the study, there is no strong evidence for a differing distribution of the forms of change occurring. The most straightforward interpretation is that all countries have the same distribution of change, they simply differ in the degree that they have them as an overall pattern. England and The Netherlands, and the private sector in France, appear to have the changes in more comprehensive forms. This in turn can be related to nations with historically more developed private sectors being more exposed to unavoidable demands for change in global economies, and a concern to manage public sector provision with a tightening of their resourcing base.

The overall conclusion however is that the nature of MM is not changing fundamentally in the way described and predicted by much of the normative literature, in these 'ordinary' organizations. Middle managers are not becoming more involved in forming strategy, they are being required to understand it better so as to implement it with less close supervision. They have looser and larger roles in terms of external constraint, but they are tightly disciplined by commitment to, and understanding of, strategy and business priorities. They are developing and using more complex 'soft' skills of people management, but in the service of performance management rather than a radical move to devolution and empowerment. Information technology is present in MM work, and may have played a part in business restructurings affecting the numbers of MMs in the past, but it is not radically affecting MM's central work in the middle of a human command chain.

In terms of effectiveness, the conclusion has to be that, as currently constituted, MM effectiveness is a development of its traditional form: translating strategy into operations, managing the change that this implies and overseeing the performance management of the operational work. The new emphases in this traditional role are on a deeper awareness of, and commitment to, strategy and business purpose (as opposed to working to formal objectives deduced from strategy by, and handed down from, senior management), and increasingly subtle human skills in gaining compliance with change and performance demands in situations which are socially diversifying and in which, in general, overt authoritarian behaviour is less acceptable.

This finding is in the context of 'ordinary' organizations in relatively developed economies (Europe) where efficiency is at a premium in defending competitiveness in very large parts of the economy.

If a more radically different form of MM and MM effectiveness is to emerge it seems unlikely that it will do so from within MM practice. If such a change were to occur it is likely to be from the context of development of radically more effective organizational forms. On the other hand, and perhaps more likely, much of the discussion of radical change in MM may turn out to have been a rhetorical practice of the 1980s, yet to be explained in depth, but possibly serving the purpose of making a process of efficiency increase and work intensification more acceptable.

IMPLICATIONS FOR RESEARCH, THEORY AND PRACTICE

There is some evidence for certain common trends affecting the European MM population. It can be inferred from that some common factors are affecting European companies and also hospitals. But the degree, nature and reasons for change are not all the same, and to account for this sociological, institutional and historical characteristics of nations and sectors have to be invoked. It seems likely that some of the differences observed in our sample (for example, the importance of loyalty in Greece, power distance in France, professional expectations in the UK) relate to these characteristics. A further analysis of the changing individual and collective behaviours of MMs could usefully examine this perspective in greater depth.

Further research could also address the question of whether some of the more radical claims for change in the MM role are in fact true in some special case organizations, and may represent a pattern still to emerge in the future, or apply only in some specialist sectors, or whether they are better explained as rhetorical practices serving a mythical function of making the current reality of tight business-oriented MM more acceptable.

The divergence between rhetoric and experience, the balance of convergence and divergence in the changes that are taking place, and national/sector differences, create the conditions for confusion in MMs understanding of their own situations. There is also potential for confusion in the aims and purposes of corporate HRM/HR development policies in relation to MM, and similarly for the MM programmes of business and management schools and other institutions involved in MM development. The conclusions of this study should provide a framework against which to review these practical issues.

NOTES

1 The research reported in this Chapter was carried out under the 'Management Effectiveness' Theme of the 'European Competitiveness in a Knowledge Society' Project, contract no. ERBCHRXCT 930232 in the Human Capital Mobility Project, DG XII, Brussels. Assistance with access to the research sites and practical arrangements for the visits by Dr L. Mota de Castro (University of Porto), Dr S. Kufidu (University of Thessaloniki) and Dr Van Gils and Dr Sanders (University of Groningen) is gratefully acknowledged.

2 Data from the English hospital in the sample was collected in conjunction with an Economic and Social Science Research Council funded project on 'contracting' in the health service as part of the Contractors and Competition Programme, award no. L114251025.

REFERENCES

Ackroyd, S. (1992) 'Paradigms lost: paradise regained?', in: M.I. Reed and M. Hughes (eds) *Rethinking Organizations: New Directions in Organization Theory and Analysis*, London: Sage, 102–119.

Alvesson, M. and Willmott, H. (1992) 'On the idea of emancipation in management and organization studies', *Academy of Management Review* **17**(3): 43–64.

Berger, P.L. and Luckman T. (1966) *The Social Construction of Reality*, Harmondsworth: Penguin.

Burgoyne, J.G. (1994) 'Stakeholder analysis', in: C. Cassell and G. Symon (eds) *Qualitative Methods in Organizational and Occupational Psychology*, London: Sage.

Burgoyne, J.G. and Lorbiecki A. (1993) 'Clinicians into management: the experience in context', *Health Services Management Research* **6**(4): 248–59.

Culler, J. (1976) *Saussure*, London: Fontana.

Hofstede, G. (1980) *Culture's Consequences*, Beverly Hills, CA: Sage.

Popper, K.R. (1963) *Conjectures and Refutations: The Growth of Scientific Knowledge*, London: Routledge, 412.

Reed, M. (1989) *The Sociology of Management*, Hemel Hempstead: Harvester Wheatsheaf.

Silverman, D. (1970) *The Theory of Organizations*, London: Heinemann.

5

MIDDLE MANAGEMENT IN CRISIS: WHO SHOULD BE BLAMED?

The French situation

Jean-Pierre Segal

Within French firms which are involved in a process of change of their management many complaints can be heard about an embarassing issue: middle managers. 'If only we had "real managers" (instead of the ones we have now), we would be better off !' Many executives seem to consider this intermediate level as a major hindrance to the process of modernization of the hierarchical structure. Their more common diagnosis insists on a so-called 'middle managers lack of skill and motivation' and asks the human resources department to build new recruitment and training programmes in order to solve the problem.

This chapter proposes a different picture of the present situation of French middle managers. Their uneasiness with their role and their very cautious behaviour towards change are analysed as the visible symptoms of a larger issue which deals with their difficulty to obtain the recognition they need to fulfil their new objectives. The building of their own legitimacy (Weber, 1922) becomes a crucial issue for these middle managers when they are not only asked to use their knowledge and to supervise their staff but also to co-ordinate their efforts and to sustain their (hoped) dedication to the organization (Dopson, Newell, et al., 1994).

Our approach is different from the classical human resources analysis which pays special attention to the training and reward of middle management, though we do admit the importance of the issue and the existence of continous efforts in these areas within the firms we have studied. Similarly, we do not ascribe to the bargaining power given (or not given) to the middle managers as much importance as the strategic approach gives to it (Crozier and Friedberg, 1977), though we have frequently identified at this level of the organization a paradoxical gap between the objectives and the means given to middle managers. This importance given to the notion of role is probably influenced by the French cultural context where the defence of one's personal status and the struggle for a higher social position are issues of great importance (de Tocqueville, 1835–40; d'Iribarne, 1989).

The present chapter is based on the conclusions of eleven case studies we have made during the last five years within large firms belonging to the public sector: four studies within the national railroad company, four studies within the Parisian public transport company and three within an industrial firm of the aeronautic sector. Three hundred semi-directive interviews were carried out, the first third with first-level supervisors, the second third with their subordinates and the other third with their superiors.

This sample should not however be considered as representative of the huge diversity of situations that can be found within French firms where the work-force is more and more employed in smaller structures than those to which we had access. Our sample is only composed of large companies, belonging to the public sector. These firms have 'produced' this numerous intermediary hierarchy for many years through internal promotions, a population which is expected today to adapt to organizational changes. The importance of the organizational changes introduced, as well as the social context, is different from one firm to the other.

Within the railroad company, local managers are facing a significant cut in the work-force and a great uncertainty about the future. As yet their role has not evolved significantly but the fact that major changes are being introduced is a source of perplexity and worry among the intermediate hierarchy. A large-scale decentralization is at the moment being carried out within the Parisian public transport firm which produces new opportunities for middle managers operating in operational units. Some of them have been in their new roles for three to five years. The industrial aeronautic company has radically changed its organizational model in order to adapt itself to market competition. The hierarchical structure has been reduced. Middle managers have become more accountable for the results of their units. Meanwhile the company has reduced drastically its staff, at each level of the hierarchy.

The first section of the chapter examines the different views expressed by this intermediate hierarchy on their past, present and future situation. This will help us to understand the diversity of their interpretation of their new role which influences their present hopes and fears towards it, a dimension which is essential to the understanding of this category. The second section reviews the different criticisms expressed by the other actors of the organization (their superiors, the managers of the other departments with whom they co-operate, their own subordinates) on the way these middle managers fulfil the (new) roles. A third section examines the organizational disfunctioning and paradoxes which should be considered, in our view, as more significant explanations of the present difficulties than the limits of skill and/or lack of motivation of the 'middle managers'. Through this analysis of the diversity of the representations of the new managerial role among the different categories involved, this chapter highlights larger social and organizational issues such as the change of authority patterns and the difficult insertion of new generation within firms. They will be discussed in the conclusion of the chapter.

LISTENING TO THE MIDDLE MANAGERS

The feelings of the intermediate hierarchy towards the change process they are willingly or unwillingly involved in are highly contradictory. On the one hand, they seem relieved by the introduction of substantial changes. One cannot clearly understand their present situation without considering their former difficulties. The uneasiness of today should not hide the problems experienced yesterday. Many of them seem to be happy with the fact of receiving much more information on the new goals of the organization and more support and attention from their superiors than they ever had before when they frequently were the 'forgotten elements' of the system. Some of them are beginning to realize that their new role could give them a strategic position within the firm, if only they can manage to make the grade. On the other hand, they seem worried by the uncertainty which threatens the new pattern of the organization and anxious about their own future. Due to their former minor position their self-assurance is often weak. Many among them believe that their superiors are not telling them the whole truth about the future of their category.

The vision of the past and the future of the organization varies from one 'middle manager' to the other. This intermediate hierarchy has been largely transformed during the last two decades, mainly through the improved education of those who have been hired at this level of the organization. Whereas, a generation ago, most of the intermediate hierarchy began its career at the bottom of the organization, climbing step by step through internal promotion, many new middle managers were hired externally, bringing new skills and new ideas, to the organization. To what extent is the same vision of the past, the present and the future common to them all (Klein, 1982)?

Three generations of middle managers

What is the influence of seniority on the attitudes of the intermediate hierarchy towards change? Three different attitudes can be found among this population.

The older managers, and especially those who have reached the ultimate step of their career, feel easy with talking about change they know they will not experience themselves. They do not hesitate to criticize the contradictions or paradoxes of the present situation. Internal changes, however, are generally considered by them as the unavoidable consequences of the evolution coming from 'outside' and which, in their view, is to take the blame.

The mid-career middle managers seem to be those who feel the most uncomfortable with the present changes. Having worked in the former system, they have not yet reached all their objectives as far as internal promotion is concerned. They suddenly have to reconsider their position in relation to their organization, at the same time keeping in mind that they will not automatically get all the benefits of many years of service. On the contrary, they may feel themselves to be in a less competitive position in relation to those who will be hired and trained to take the new roles for which the former are unprepared.

The younger generation is at least well aware of the rules of the new game. Many young middle managers know that the former system of rules and seniority left them only limited opportunity of being promoted in the near future. The new system can encourage their professional achievement. However, other recently recruited middle managers, especially those who had joined these large public organizations looking for job security and a guaranteed career, may feel disappointed and share the feelings of the older generation.

Looking for an exit door

Whether they are junior or senior members of the intermediate hierarchy, middle managers find it increasingly more difficult to adapt themselves to the slowly developing crisis which threatens the stability of their position. This crisis can be described through three dimensions:

1   The first dimension is a matter of professional identity. Middle managers experience an identity crisis, linked mainly with the increasing distance between the traditional image of their category and its new profile. Instead of the faithful servants of the bureaucracy promoted through seniority, one may meet currently an incoming generation which is younger, more educated than the former and which no longer believes they owe anything to the organization which has promoted them. While the difference between them and the workers beneath them in the organizational structure is increasing, they have not enough qualifications nor experience to be considered socially as full members of the managing staff.
2   Meanwhile, these new middle managers are often located at the bottom of large bureaucracies where they cannot take any initiative. They are facing a professional crisis, imputable to the increasing gap between what middle managers actually were asked to do and what they felt they were able to perform or what they were expecting to do before joining the firm.
3   Last but not least, middle managers experience an authority crisis due to the obsolescence of the traditional pattern of command which exposes them to growing difficulties in being obeyed. Their situation is all the more uneasy because they do not approve (and generally do not use) the official discipline procedures but are not in a position to introduce new methods more adapted to their expectations and those of their staff.

This situation had in the recent past created different behaviours among this population. While some of them were still conforming to the traditional rules and standards, others distanced themselves from an organization which, they believed, was unable to provide them with a real professional challenge.

The introduction of change within these bureaucratic structures has had a twofold effect on this intermediate hierarchy: on the one hand, some of these middle managers may have thought this offer was coming too late and that resistance to change could be an effective way to keep the comfortable distance they have established between the organization and themselves; on the other hand, the managerial offer may have been considered a unique opportunity to escape from an uncomfortable position.

LISTENING TO THE CRITICS

How do middle managers, as seen by the other members of the organization, perform in their new role? Are their superiors and their subordinates more (or less) satisfied with their contribution? What do the representatives of the other departments say about their efficiency in their new tasks of 'co-ordinating'? Are these different views convergent or divergent? Are the middle managers in a position to satisfy and convince the other members of the organization whose requirements are generally different and sometimes contradictory?

The upper management view

Listening to the superiors of the (new) middle managers gives to the observer a rather disappointing view of those who were supposed to carry on their shoulders most of the innovative projects of the organization (participative management, quality management, decentralized human resource management and management control). Naturally, these superiors have to admit that middle managers need time and training for their new tasks. They generally try to moderate their views in order to preserve their relationship with these middle managers whose help they need to reach their own objectives. But they cannot hide their animosity towards those middle managers who do not fulfil their expectations.

Two main criticisms are expressed towards middle managers by their superiors: one against their skill, the other against their behaviour.

1 'We have not chosen them and we have to live with them' is a sentence one may frequently hear from the superior of these new middle managers. However, the original bureaucratic rules governing to whom they are expected to delegate new responsibilities have rarely been changed. The day-to-day confusion between the function and the status of the bureaucratic staffs has, moreover, frequently led candidates to apply to 'managers positions' not only unprepared but also unfit for this role. This situation can be found especially within the two railway and public transport companies where middle managers have been promoted on the basis of their technical knowledge rather than on their ability to manage people.

2 The way these middle managers fulfil their duties is also much criticized, not only by their superiors but also by the managers of the departments who rely on the effectiveness of their management. Two points are generally made contesting the way middle managers organize their time and face responsibilities in tough situations. How do the (new) middle managers define their priorities among the various tasks they have to complete? Do they have a clear understanding of what is the most important and what can wait, what they should delegate and what they should do themselves? The answers to these questions are generally negative. For their superiors, middle managers cannot organize their time efficiently enough because they have not really appropriated their new roles, even when they 'perform' for the sake of appearances.

The quality of their work, the attention they pay to following day-to-day operations suffer from this situation. If one wishes to develop the analysis, it may be considered that (many) middle managers have not yet managed to clearly understand the finalities of their new position which is, in the mind of their superiors, to serve the new objectives of the organization through providing positive support given to the rank and file. On the contrary, they are accused of a misappropriation of their new prerogatives: middle managers select among the numerous tasks they are given the ones they feel most comfortable with (and with a larger expectation of personal benefit), neglecting the others; middle managers have better networking with the other middle managers than checking the individual performance of their staff.

This point is closely linked to the other side of the criticism which denounces middle managers' uneasiness facing responsibility. The following words sum up the disappointment of their superior: 'as long as they have not to decide by themselves, they look autonomous; but as soon as the situation becomes difficult, their former dependence on their hierarchy reappears'. Cultural inheritance of risk aversion and dependence on authority are generally indicated by upper management as possible explanations for such behaviour. This psychological rather than organizational view leads directly to coping with the problem in terms of education and training, a solution which has the great advantage of being practical if not always efficient.

The views of the rank and file

If there was a strong convergence in the criticisms expressed by the upper management towards the so-called 'new field management', a large diversity of attitudes may be found among their subordinates, with a clear contrast between the views of the older and the younger generations.

The older generation

The older generation still believes in the traditional system in which the manager has to share the skills and the working conditions of the staff under his or her command in order to legitimate his or her authority. They find it hard to believe the usefulness of the various meetings which their boss attends. Modern management is considered by them to be a passing fad.

Whether a manager belongs to the older or the newer generation, it seems difficult for him or her to build credibility in the eyes of the experienced workers: in the first situation, he or she generally shares the same past with the rank and file, who have kept in mind their former practices of management; in the second situation, the young new managers are considered not only too dependent on the view of the upper management but also too socially and professionally different from the rank and file.

85

The new generation

The attitude of the younger generation seems more positive, at least towards the young middle managers. Whereas the older staff appreciate a manager with a similar professional background, the younger staff seem less concerned with this dimension. Only a small proportion of the younger staff have been trained through the classical apprenticeship system. The average new recruit has received a longer general education. He or she has grown up within a 'bargaining culture' and is expecting to establish with their professional hierarchy a relation similar to the ones they have with their parents or teachers.

The intermediate hierarchy is empirically trying to implement the appropriate way to manage this new generation. As long as they control the right levers to answer the needs of their staff, they can develop a relationship which may satisfy both sides. But as soon as they reach the limits of their influence, their authority is exposed to be considerably reduced. The new generation has no respect for intermediate staff who need always to 'report' to someone above them before answering a question. They do not hesitate to bypass the official hierarchy in order to join the relevant interlocutor.

The shadow of the real boss

Who is the 'real boss'? Great importance is given in the French cultural context to this question. Because he or she has to behave as an arbitrator, the French chief needs to keep a certain distance between him or herself and the staff. A higher status and a strong personal legitimacy are requisites for building the credibility of this figurehead and the respect he or she may inspire (Segal, 1987).

As long as the deputy manager is merely seen as an assistant of the 'real' manager, the former may benefit from the strong position of his or her superior, even if his or her secondary position may suggest some irony among the staff. As soon as this deputy manager is put into a fully responsible manager's position, which is much more exposed, he or she has to satisfy a higher standard of personal legitimacy. Some in this position may not fulfil this standard when they are still considered the 'little helpers' of the 'real chief'.

DOES THE ORGANIZATION REALLY SUPPORT MIDDLE MANAGERS?

How should we interpret these criticisms towards middle management? Listening to the middle managers taught us that most of them were willing to examine the idea of changing their role. The explanation in terms of unwillingness or resistance to change are not as convincing as upper management generally believe. Fear of contributing to the reduction of the employment of their own category does exist in public structures where, for historical reasons, the intermediate hierarchy has been considerably inflated in order to open career paths to the rank and file. Yet the argument explains better the anxiety towards the future than the present difficulties in the implementation of the new role.

Does the organization, as it works today, really help middle managers to fulfil their new role? The different data we have collected during the last five years suggest a negative answer to this question with three criticisms to address to the organization on the way middle managers are themselves oriented and managed:

1 The model of management which middle managers are asked to implement does not always fit either the reality of their context of work or the nature of the work itself. This dimension explains a large part of the doubt middle managers may have on the efficiency and on the effectiveness of their management.

2 The support that middle managers could expect from their own hierarchy is rarely provided, a fact that is in obvious contradiction with the principles middle managers themselves are asked to apply towards their subordinates. This point is closely linked with the feelings of unfairness and hypocrisy frequently expressed by middle managers.

3 Very little is generally done either to build the understanding of the new role of 'field manager' or to strengthen the personal legitimacy of the managers themselves. These two issues are nevertheless crucial in order to give to the new field managers the visibility and the credibility they often lack. The point is all the more crucial in large public structure where these 'new managers' are seen as the heirs of the former hierarchy.

Does the managerial model always fit the middle managers' work reality?

A recent comparison between German and British first-line managers (Ganter, 1993) provides an interesting view on the contrast between two models of management. The Anglo-Saxon managerial model grants high value to flexibility and adaptability to the market, and is customer and budget oriented. The model has two implicit bases: there is always a customer to satisfy through a better adjustment between the present resources of the organization and the customers' requirements; there is a group of operators headed by a manager. Within this model, the manager is accountable for the financial results of his or her units (which shows his or her adaptability to the market) and should dispose of large-scale devolution of authority (including hiring of staff) in order to take the decisions as close as possible to the budget and the market. Meanwhile this manager is also responsible for training and the motivating of his or her staff. The manager is supposed to be the interpreter of the customers' needs.

The German professional model is more oriented towards the development of the skill of his or her staff and the quality of the production. The field management has to be delegated to highly trained professionals whose legitimacy is founded on skill and pedagogy. He or she is not asked to 'change' the organization but to develop its technical strength and help, through this professional excellence, a commercial performance which does not rely on the manager.

The French situation, at least within the three firms we have analysed, is traditionally more inspired by the professional system (d'Iribarne, 1994). It finds difficulty however, in developing a co-ordination between the different professions and gives a greater emphasis on the decision role of the upper management held by engineers (whereas the German 'Meister' has a larger role than its French counterpart).

The process of decentralization and a growing dependence towards the market economy (vs the public demand) have introduced a radical change: the Anglo-Saxon model of a market-oriented management is actively promoted, being considered a remedy against bureaucratic centralization and against the old routines of self-centred organizations. Yet the question whether this fashionable model really fits the reality of the work at the bottom of the organization has generally never been explored by those who define the managerial strategy at the head of the firm.

Middle managers, probably more than any other actors within the organization, are the ones who will have to live with this limited coherence between theory and its application. The cases of the rail companies, either the national or the Parisian one, teach us how difficult it is to implement a managerial model within a reality where there are very few strong work units, having instead a large majority of situations of isolated work within shifts whose schedules are generally different from those of the field supervisor, now promoted to a managerial position. Where is the added value of a managerial actor in charge of giving 'adaptability' to his or her unit within such a professional universe structured by so obvious technical and social contingencies. Meanwhile there is a crucial need to protect the authority of the persons in charge from the criticisms we have mentioned of incompetence or inefficiency, especially in the case where the traditional model of technical expertise, which had hitherto produced the legitimacy of the local management, would be significantly changed.

Decentralization and local management

A second point that should be mentioned for the 'defence' of those middle managers, who are so often criticized, is the (under-standable) instability and non-fulfilment of the decentralization process which was supposed to be the framework of the middle manager's work. This situation produced the following consequences in every case we have studied:

1 The upper level of management, which is supposed not only to give goals and guidelines to the middle managers but also to follow up their work and identify their assistance or coaching requirements, very rarely fulfils these engagements. This common situation is more often the consequence of a lack of time than a pure lack of interest (even if such behaviour does exist). The defence of their territory or the strategic use of the new opportunities created by the decentralization process mobilize all their energy at the expense of the lower levels.

2 The more the decentralization process advances towards the lower levels of the organization, the fewer additional prerogatives are distributed to the local managers and the wider the gap becomes between job description and real content of the function. The distance taken from the field of operations, criticized by the rank and file, can be interpreted as a result of an avoidance strategy from the local managers who feel they should develop a horizontal strategy (through networking activities, for instance) rather than directly interfering with the work of their subordinates (avoiding the risk of being asked questions they cannot answer).

A need for a better insertion

The introduction of a new role within the organization should not be considered without paying attention to its content (in terms of new tasks and new objectives) and its insertion within the existing social structure. It could be argued that creating a new role implies a strong will to change the organization (and, perhaps a new social system) and this has to deal with the effects of the disturbance introduced. The field data we have collected leads to a different analysis, indicating the extreme importance of building a new legitimacy for the new role as well as for the new incomers (the middle managers).

1 Legitimacy for the role itself is not as obvious as one may believe, anticipating the expected organizational benefits. Within a technical environment, such as industry or transport, the major local uncertainty is not generally the customers' behaviour but the technical control of the process and the work security of the staff. Greater legitimacy will be given to the local managers who will be able to contribute positively to these major issues. The good profile of the local manager, in accordance with the specificities of the work process and its environment, still remains a (sometimes forgotten) basis of a good local management.

2 Building personal legitimacy for the local manager is a second issue whose importance has been underestimated in the French cultural context. Whereas in the Anglo-Saxon culture, the legitimacy of a manager is strongly associated with his or her accountability (he or she is supposed to assume the results

of the unit he or she has in charge), the French culture insists on the individual legitimacy and its congruence with the social status associated with the function. This dimension introduces frequent difficulties for middle managers whose personal status is not judged high enough for the new position of manager or those whose former experience or educational background are considered as irrelevant to their new responsibilty.

Building this legitimacy has been conceived traditionally through the definition of educational and career paths to prepare the incomer for this new responsibility. The time needed to implement such a solution is generally not anticipated. Present uneasiness of many middle managers has much to do with this dimension.

CONCLUSION: MIDDLE MANAGERS' DISCOMFORT AS A SYMPTOM

Local managers are often described as reluctant to become involved with employees' involvement or organizational change. This interpretation of their behaviour may please their superiors and (occasionally) their subordinates. It has not been yet confirmed by the data we have collected. When uneasiness with and/or reluctance to the changes proposed by the upper management can be verified among local managers, (a situation which is common), explanations other than their 'archaism' or their 'bad temper' should be considered in order to analyse their attitudes and behaviours.

This chapter explores two different research tracks. The first track (mentioned in the first section) is a socio-cultural one. It proposed considering local managers not as the rearguard who finds it hard to follow the modernization process (even if such categories can be identified) but as the advance guard of a new generation which will in the future join large bureaucratic firms with an educational and cultural background very different from the former generation. This new generation is developing a higher level of expectation as regards the content of their work due to a longer education, a lower ambition of social promotion within a job which is rarely their first choice in an economic context of lasting unemployment and a strong reluctance to generate discipline conflict with their subordinates who will frequently. behave in a similar way.

The second track (developed in the third section) is a socio-organizational one. An organizational model which is generally proposed (at least within our sample) cannot be implemented without substantial adaptation to the technical and social local context of work. Middle managers not only need training and support from their hierarchy, they also have to earn local recognition, a social process which takes longer than is thought at first.

REFERENCES

Crozier, M. and, Friedberg, E., (1977) *L'acteur et le système*, Paris: Seuil.

Dopson, S., Newell H. and Neumann J. (1994) 'Middle manager's reaction to their changing contracts', communication to the Lyon Conference. See Chapter 10 of this book.

Ganter, H.D. (1993) 'Problems of transferring managerial knowledge: lessons from a cross-cultural comparison', 11th EGOS Colloquium, Paris.

d'Iribarne, P.(1989) *La logique de l'honneur*, Paris: Seuil.

— (1994) 'The honour principle in the 'bureaucratic phenomenon', *Organizations Studies*, **1**.

Klein, J. (1982) 'Why do supervisors resist employees' involvement', *Harvard Business Review*, **5**, September–October.

Segal, J.-P. (1987), 'Le prix de la légitimité hiérarchique', in *Gérer et Comprendre, Annales des Mines*, June.

de Tocqueville, A. (1981),*De la democratie en Amerique*, Paris: Garnier-Flammarion.

Weber, M. (1922) *Economie et Société*, 2 vols, Paris: Plon.

6

THE NATURE OF MIDDLE MANAGERS' WORK IN THE CIVIL SERVICE

The case of Greece

Stella Kufidu, Eugenia Petridu and Dimitrios M. Mihail

INTRODUCTION

In the face of large-scale pressures for change, including intensified and international competition, developments in information and manufacturing technologies, and work-force expectations, organizations in the private and public sector have responded in different ways. In the private sector, restructuring and a more efficient utilization of human resources has been the common response.

Along the same lines the public sector seems to be pursuing an 'efficiency strategy' encouraging the development of flexible and customer-oriented organizations. Emphasis has been placed on reorganizing public management through new technologies and 'empowering managers' in order to meet the customers' expectations (Gore, 1994; Dopson et al. 1991, 1993; Howard, 1993; Hyde, 1992; McIntoch, 1990; Metcalfe and Richards 1990; Nutt and Backolf, 1993; Peters and Savoie, 1994; Shoop, 1991; Skelcher, 1992; Storey and Fenwick, 1990; Wagenheim and Reurintt 1991).

In the context of these changes middle managers' work, attitudes and skills have been particularly affected. It has been argued that middle managers will engage in new roles such as those of facilitator, coach, innovator or leader, suppressing their traditional role as commanders and controllers. Evidence

93

suggests that middle managers' jobs have become more general with greater responsibilities, more accountability and an increased span of control. Moreover, the need for middle managers to develop advanced conceptual abilities and participation in strategic-decision-making has been realized (Goffee and Scase 1986; Kanter, 1982, 1986; Schilit, 1987; Torrington and Weightman 1987).

Post-war Greek public services have been facing rigid structures characterized by client relationships between citizens and the parties in power, extensive bureaucracy and inefficient management (Argiropoulou, 1987, 1990; Dekleris and Karkatsoulis, 1994; Makridimitris, 1990; Papadimitriou and Makridimitris 1991; Theophanidis, 1992.). All these drawbacks have led to mediocrity, a lack of motivated personnel and an inability to meet citizens' expectations. Since 1986 institutional reforms have been put forward to overcome the above-mentioned shortcomings and upgrade the Greek civil service. A series of institutional arrangements (laws 1599/86, 1892/90, 1943/91, 2000/91, 2085/92, 2026/94), have focused on decentralizing and simplifying bureaucratic procedures and on reforming personnel management policies. In the midst of these adjustments the role of managers in the civil service should be of utmost importance.

METHODOLOGY

Our study is an attempt to investigate the role of Greek middle-level managers in the public services. The objective of our chapter is to examine (a) the content of middle managers' work by assessing their activities and (b) if changes related to their activities have been observed as a result of the reforms introduced.

Our study was carried out in Northern Greece among sixty-two middle managers employed in several departments of seven ministries. The sample was drawn from middle managers who participated in training programmes offered by the National Centre for Public Management in Thessaloniki. Data were collected by means of a structured questionnaire that was completed anonymously by the participating managers. They were asked to assess the structure of their activities as well as their authority and their perceptions of the extent of the changes which have occurred, and should occur, in relation to their activities. Perceptions were measured on a seven-point scale and the main ratings are illustrated in the figures in the text. Ratings referring to preferred levels of managerial activities, are presented with dotted columns in the figures. This method was applied because it allowed managers to respond avoiding any work environment distraction.

FINDINGS

Middle managers' activities and authority

The first concern of our survey was to detect the extent to which middle-level managers are involved in their managerial activities. We approached this issue by examining the time devoted to managerial functions and the authority they possessed. Research evidence indicates that managers in the public sector perform the same kind of activities as managers in the private sector in terms of complexity of job content (Gerding and Sevenjuijsen, 1987: 115; Lau and Pavett, 1980).

A considerable amount of research has been devoted to middle managers' work, focusing on classifying their activities into different groupings (Mintzberg, 1973; Torrington and Weightman, 1982; Carroll and Gillen, 1987). In this context the classical functions still seem to represent a widely accepted way of conceptualizing their work (Carroll and Gillen, 1987). However, emphasis has been given to middle managers' activities, underlining 'linking groups' (planning and allocating resources, co-ordinating, managing group performance – Kraut et al., 1989), and 'participating in strategy process and planning' (Wooldridge and Floyd, 1990; Wesley, 1990).

Data referring to the distribution of time devoted to middle managers' activities indicate that a considerable amount of their working time is still absorbed in routine and control activities. Indeed, as Figure 6.1 shows almost one-third of their time (28 per cent) is spent on routine paperwork, followed by the activity of controlling/correcting subordinates' work (18 per cent). This means that only about half of their time is devoted to routine administrative tasks. As expected, only the other half is spent on managerial activities such as co-ordinating, directing and developing subordinates, work programming and organizing. It is apparent that Greek middle managers in the public services are largely involved in bureaucratic activities.

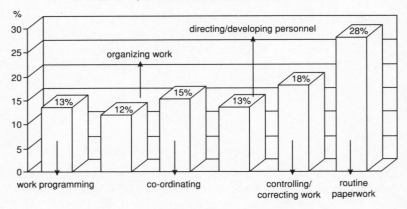

Figure 6.1 Middle managers' distribution of time

Closely related to managerial activities is the issue of middle managers' authority. Research evidence suggests that their authority both in the private and public sector is considered to be insufficient, uncertain and disproportionate to the responsibilities assigned (Dekleris and Karkatsoulis, 1994; Dopson and Stewart, 1990; Kay, 1974; Nutt and Backolf 1993; Solomon, 1986; Spanou, 1992; Theophanidis, 1992).

The findings of our survey seem to support these views, as participants reported limited authority. This inclusive finding is supported by more specific ones. As Figure 6.2 shows, middle managers' authority in managing human resources seems to be very limited. In particular, participants reported that their ability to impose penalties or offer rewards to subordinates is very low. However, the fragmented authority in controlling rewards or penalties seems to be due mainly to bureaucratic constraints and the extensive use of formal regulations which characterize public management. It should also be noticed that basic organizational principles, such as unity of command, seem to be violated. These findings could be regarded as strongly diminishing their power in managing people effectively. It is quite optimistic that middle managers believe that they should be granted more authority.

An unexpected finding was the moderate authority that middle managers possess concerning their immediate subordinates' performance appraisal. Provided that the desired rating

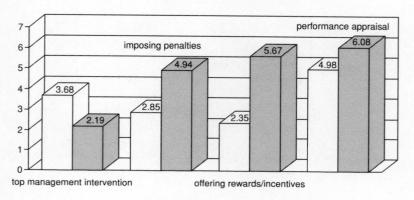

Figure 6.2 Middle managers' authority

on this issue was very high, it is apparent that their involvement in this procedure should be more decisive.

As Figure 6.3 shows, the involvement of middle managers in the organization's and the department's long- and short-term planning, as well as work organizing or affecting the functioning of the department, appears to lack the dynamics necessary for empowering them.

From the above discussion one would conclude that even though half of their time is presumably devoted to no bureaucratic activities, the preconditions for pursuing these activities effectively are not sound.

Changes reported in middle managers' role and work

In this section we attempt to investigate if changes related to middle managers' work have been observed as a result of the recent institutional reforms introduced in the public services. To this end in our survey middle managers assessed the extent to which changes have been observed and those that should have occurred. These changes were similar to those referred to in the literature (Dopson et al., 1991; Dopson and Stewart, 1990, 1993; Gore, 1994; Jackson and Humble, 1994; Rainey et al., 1976; Skelcher, 1992; Strand, 1987; Weiss, 1988; Whorton and Worthlay 1981).

Changes have been grouped into two categories:

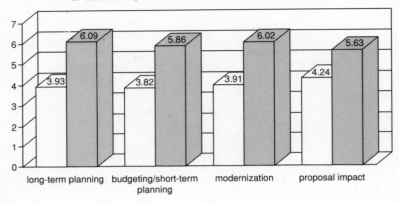

Figure 6.3 Participation in decision-making

- changes in government policies concerning the development of managers' roles in the public services
- associated organizational changes in middle managers' work.

Figure 6.4 depicts managers' perceptions of changes in government policies related to the development of their roles.

The core of public management adjustment consisted of the introduction of new technology, the reduction of bureaucracy, incentive rewards and performance appraisal objectiveness for managers in the public services. It seems that changes regarding main policies which affect the managers work and, in turn, their role have been remarkably slight. By contrast, the 'necessity for change' appears to be of considerable importance for all policies examined, as reported by participants. The lack of motivation and reward schemes, the insufficient performance appraisal mechanisms, the scourge of bureaucracy as well as the lack of momentum in the application of new technology have been indicated as being the predominant problems of Greek public management. Based on these findings, one would maintain that these disappointing developments tend to discourage a more efficient utilization of managerial skills. Within this framework expectations of a qualitative leap in viewing middle managers in the public services as 'facilitator', 'coach', 'innovator' or 'leader' are not well grounded. Indeed, findings regarding changes in the main aspects of middle managers' work – shown in Figures 6.5 and 6.6 – support our contention.

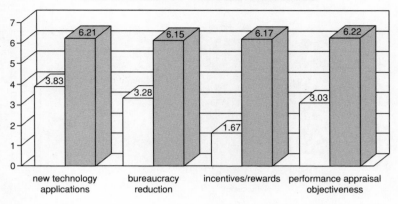

Figure 6.4 Perceived changes in policies related to the development of managers' roles

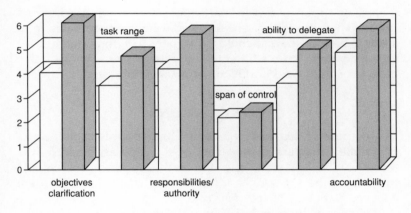

Figure 6.5 Perceived changes in middle managers' activities: 1

The conclusion that can be drawn is that the extent to which changes have occurred is moderate. However, the crucial finding is that these changes, according to the opinion of the partici- pants, have not been as bold as they should have been. A closer look at the factors studied shows that the 'demand for change' is astonishingly high for 'routine paperwork reduction', 'more clearly specified objectives', 'greater accountability', 'more authority and responsibility' and 'more delegation'. Changes

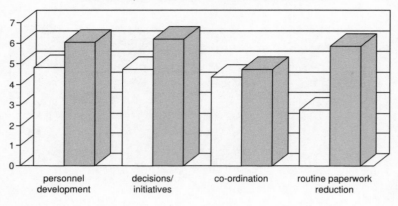

Figure 6.6 Perceived changes in middle managers' activities: 2

regarding opportunities to 'participate in decision-making and undertake more initiatives' or to 'develop subordinates' also seem to be moderate. It could be argued, therefore, that middle managers seem to be willing to suppress routine administrative aspects of their work in favour of managerial ones.

CONCLUSIONS

The purpose of this study was to attempt to investigate the role of middle managers in the Greek public services, based on the activities they perform and the authority they possess. At the same time we sought to assess the changes which were believed to have affected their role.

Our survey indicated that middle managers in the public services are heavily engaged in routine administrative tasks at the expense of managerial ones. The latter are probably limited by their lack of authority in setting rewards, imposing penalties and participating in departmental planning and organizing. The source of these inefficiencies should be found in the fragmented adjustments in the Greek civil service. Indeed recent research raises relevant critique emphasizing the lack of broad reforms addressing basic organizational issues. Among the most important are considered the overlapping of departmental objectives, the *ad hoc* political intervention in the structure and the organization of the civil service, and the existing client relationships

100

overwhelming the recruitment process. Under these circumstances one could doubt if managers with vague objectives, lacking new technology, struggling with bureaucratic procedures, and lacking any motivation for better performance and reward are allowed to take initiatives and contribute to the readjustment of public management to meet citizens' expectations.

It is apparent that bolder, more radical arrangements should be introduced, adjusting the whole institutional framework to the imperatives of flexible customer-oriented public organizations. Policy measures should be primarily oriented towards establishing an arm's length relationship between political power and public management; clarifying organization's mission and disentangling departmental objectives; empowering managers by restructuring their job content and utilizing managers' skills by motivating better performance. Expectations of improving public management in the next decade are grounded not only in the emergence of a new institutional setting *per se* but also in the ability of Greece to embrace it by an 'efficiency strategy' and effectively adjust it to the environment of the European Union.

REFERENCES

Argiropoulou, A. (1987) *State-Public Interrelation*, Athens: (n.p.).
— (1990) *The Role of Public Administration in the Process of Development*, Athens: National Centre for Public Management.
Carroll, S. and Gillen, D. (1987) 'Are the classical management functions useful in describing managerial work?', *Academy of Management Review* 12(1): 38–51.
Dekleris, M. and Karkatsoulis, P.(1994) Restructuring and clarifying public services' mission, unpublished report.
Dopson, S., Risk, A. and Stewart, R. (1991) 'The changing role of the middle manager in the United Kingdom', *International Studies of Management and Organization* 22(1): 40–53.
Dopson, S. and Stewart, R. (1990) 'Public and private sector management: the case for a wider debate', *Public Money and Management* 10(1): 37–40.
— (1993) 'Information technology organizational restructuring and the future of middle management', *New Technology, Work and Employment* 8(1): 10–20.
Dunaine, B. (1993) 'The non-managers', *Fortune* 127(4): 38–42.
Gerding, G. and Sevenjuijsen, R.F. (1987) *Public Manager in the Middle*, in J.I. Kooiman and K.A. Eliasen (eds) *Managing Public Organizations: Lessons from Contemporary European Experience*, London: Sage.
Goffee, R. and Scase, R. (1986) 'Are the rewards worth the effort? Changing Managerial Values in the 1980s', *Personnel Review* 15(4): 36.

Gore, A. Jr (1994) 'The new job of the federal executive', *Public Administration Review* **54**(4): 317–21.

Howard, G. (1993) 'Organizational change in local government: a role for activity analysis', *Management Services* **37**(9): 18–23

Hyde, A. (1992) 'The proverbs of total quality management: recharting the path to quality improvement in the public sector', *Public Productivity and Management Review* **XVI**(1): 25–37.

Jackson, D. and Humble, J. (1994) 'Middle managers: new purpose, new directions', *Journal of Management Development* **13**(3): 15–21.

Kanter, R.M. (1982) 'The middle manager as innovator', *Harvard Business Review* **60**(4): 95–105.

—— (1986) 'The reshaping of middle management', *Management Review* **75**(1): 19–20.

Kay, E. (1974) 'Middle Management', in J. O'Toole (ed.) *Work and Quality of Life*, Cambridge, MA: MIT Press.

Kraut, A., Pedigo, P.R., McKenna, D. and Dunnette, D. (1989) 'The role of the manager: what's really important in different management jobs', *The Academy of Management Executive* **III**(4): 286–93.

Lau, A. and Pavett, C. (1980) 'The nature of managerial work: a comparison of public and private sector managers', *Group and Organization Studies* **5**(4): 453–66.

McIntosh, S. (1990) 'Clerical jobs in transition', *Human Resource Magazine* **35**(9): 70–72.

Makridimitris, A. (1990) 'Management development in public administration: an integrated model for improving management capacity, *Bulletin of Business Administration*, **29**(259); 31–6; (261); 47–50; (262); 43–49.

Metcalfe, L. and Richards, S. (1990) *Improving Public Management*, London: European Institute of Public Administration and Sage.

Mintzberg, H. (1973) *The Nature of Managerial Work*, New York: Prentice Hall.

Nutt, P. and Backolf, R. (1993) 'Transforming public organizations with strategic management and strategic leadership', *Journal of Management* **19**(2): 299–347.

Papadimitriou, G. and Makridimitris, A. (1991) *Modernization in Public Management*, Athens: Sakkoulas.

Peters, B. and Savoie, D. (1994) 'Civil service reform: misdiagnosing the patient', *Public Administration Review* **54**(5): 418–25.

Rainey, M., Backolf, R. and Levine, C. (1976) 'Comparing public and private organizations', *Public Administration Review* **36**(2): 233–44.

Schilit, K. (1987) 'An examination of the influence of middle-level managers in formulating and implementing strategic decisions', *Journal of Management Studies* **24**(3): 271–93.

Shoop, T. (1991) 'Uphill climb to quality', *Government Executive* **23**(3): 17–19.

Skelcher, C. (1992) 'Improving the quality of local public services', *The Service Industries Journal* **12**(4): 463–77.

Solomon, E. (1986) 'Private and public sector managers: an empirical investigation of job characteristics and organizational climate', *Journal of Applied Psychology* **71**(2): 247–59.

Spanou, K. (1992) *Organization and Authority*, Athens: Papazisis.
Storey, J. and Fenwick, W. (1990) 'The changing face of employment management in local government', *Journal of General Management* 16(1): 14–30.
Strand, J. (1987) 'The public manager, bureaucrats or contingent actors?', in J.I. Kooniman and K.A. Eliasen (eds) *Managing Public Organizations: Lessons from Contemporary European Experience*, London: Sage.
Theophanidis, S. (1992) *Public Administration, Facing the Challenge of '1992'*, Athens: Athens Academy (preliminary report).
Torrington, D. and Weightman, J. (1987) 'Middle management work', *Journal of General Management* 13(2): 74–89.
Wagenheim, G. and Reurintt, J. (1991) 'Customer service in public administration', *Public Administration Review* 51(3): 263–9.
Weiss, R. (1988) 'Will the role of managers decline in the corporation of the future?', *National Productivity Review* 7(2): 114–21.
Wesley, F.R. (1990) 'Middle managers and strategy', *Strategic Management Journal* 11(5): 337–51.
Whorton, J. and Worthlay, J. (1981) 'A perspective on the challenge of public management: environment paradox and organizational culture', *Academy of Management Review* 6(3): 357–361.
Wooldridge, B. and Floyd S. (1990) 'The strategy process, middle management involvement', *Strategic Management Journal* 11(3): 231–241.

7

TOWARDS THE DISAPPEARANCE OF MIDDLE MANAGERS?

Three case studies in Danish knowledge organizations

Henrik Holt Larsen

INTRODUCTION

Recent changes in the European business community have increased the strategic emphasis on the human resources of organizations. This is particularly seen in knowledge-intensive and service-oriented organizations, where business strategy and human resource management (HRM) strategy tend to merge. The immaterial nature of the 'products' of knowledge organization necessitates an intensive use of high-level human competence. The HR strategy is no longer merely a passive reflection of and an adjustment to the business strategy. In reverse, the HR strategy can in fact determine the business strategy. This represents a move from 'business-driven HRM' to 'HRM-driven business'.

Intertwined with this are changing demands on middle managers. First, middle managers are playing an integrative role for downward and upward communication about strategy formulation and implementation. In this way, a (direct) line is established between the overall business strategy via departmental objectives to personal goal-setting. Second, the middle manager plays an important role in the articulation and change of organizational culture as a means of achieving organizational flexibility. Third, the match of jobs and individuals (which is an important middle manager task) has an inherent learning effect as experiential learning on the job is a powerful way of enhancing employees' competence. Finally, middle managers are to an increasing extent assigned the responsibility for dealing with a broad range of human resource issues. This chapter discusses these trends in relation to three specific Danish cases.

THE ROLE OF THE MIDDLE MANAGER IN KNOWLEDGE ORGANIZATIONS

The concept of middle management is widely discussed in other chapters of this book as well as in the literature (Borucki et al., 1992; Dopson et al., 1992; Dopson and Stewart, 1990). Hence, in this chapter we concentrate on the role of middle managers in knowledge organizations and see this role in a national culture perspective.

Unavoidably, however, this issue reflects the general development in the understanding of the concept of management over the last decades. The most significant change in the perception of management is the transition from looking at management as an individual (person-related) role, behaviour, style or method to looking at management as a process of interaction between people, some of whom can be leaders – but they don't necessarily have to be. Some substantial findings in this area are that:

- management is situationally determined, i.e., dependent upon those specific circumstances and environmental conditions under which the management is performed
- management often (and to a growing extent) is performed by teams of leaders and other key persons, instead of individual managers
- management in principle can be exerted in a social interaction between people, where none of those have to be formally appointed managers
- management materializes as the mutual interaction between a manager and the others, not the one-way impact of the manager on the non-managers
- management is culturally determined in the sense that managers can influence culture, but are often themselves victims of culture as well.

Hence, management can be interpreted as a process of interaction between individuals (of which some can be managers), taking place in a specific structural and cultural contact, and being influenced by the current situational conditions.

105

In the following section four areas of managerial tasks are presented and analysed.

The integrative role

Traditionally, most organizations have found it difficult – or not even worth while – to encircle and explicate a corporate vision and turn it into operational objectives. With a high degree of stability in market conditions, technology and organizational characteristics, the need for such overall guiding tools has been modest, and organizations have been able to continue to operate as in the past, provided that they were good at it.

However, when environmental conditions are turbulent, the competitive structure is labile and/or the technology is developing at a very fast pace, there is a strong need for: 'a process or set of processes for establishing shared understanding about what is to be achieved (and how it is to be achieved), and of managing people in a way that increases the probability that it will be achieved' (Hartle, 1992: 96). The middle manager plays a key role in contributing to the implementation (or to a lesser extent the development of) corporate vision, objectives and specific tasks (Schlesinger and Oshry, 1984). They are 'strategic ambassadors', helping to link the overall objectives and strategies of the organization with the tasks of each individual:

> The main job of managers in the knowledge-creating company is to orient this chaos toward purposeful knowledge creation. Managers do this by providing employees with a conceptual framework that helps them make sense of their own experience. This takes place at the senior management level at the top of the company and at the middle management level on company teams.
>
> Senior managers give voice to a company's future by articulating metaphors, symbols, and concepts that orient the knowledge-creating activities of employees. They do this by asking the questions: What are we trying to learn? What do we need to know? Where should we be going? Who are we? If the job of frontline employees is to know 'what is', then the job of senior executives is to know 'what ought to be'.
>
> (Nonaka, 1991: 103)

There are a number of serious concerns to be taken into consideration:

1 The deductive process from overall vision to individual objectives is presented here as a rational, carefully thought through process (or cycle). In reality, organizations tend to 'enter' the process at any given stage and go forward as well as backwards in the degree of specificity.
2 Many organizations tend to forget the first part of the process, being mainly concerned with the operational level (strategies, policies and plans).
3 The flow does not indicate how the diagnosis of the organization and the environmental conditions should be carried out (Furnham and Gunter, 1993).
4 One should not take for granted that the organization has the ability/desire to deal with vision, mission and objectives.

The argument here is that middle managers have a role to play in this vision management process. They are involved in the identification and legitimization of the *raison d'être* of the organization. They are also able to involve other stakeholders (typically the subordinates) in this process and hence judge whether changing environmental conditions make fundamental changes in the 'identity' of the organization natural or necessary.

Defining, and continually reassessing, the organizational identity includes an analysis of internal as well as external forces. The organization is not a clearly defined entity, somewhat segregated from the environment. On the contrary, the organization is an integrated part of a network, which includes customers, suppliers, public authorities, etc. In knowledge organizations, non-managerial staff (in this case knowledge workers) often have direct, intensive contact with the outside world, particularly with customers or suppliers. Hence, middle managers receive via the subordinates feedback from extra-organizational sources and transmit this information to top management (the bottom-up ambassador role). This is a supplement to the top-down ambassador role described previously.

Cultural flexibility

As mentioned above, managers are influencing, and being influenced by, the organizational culture. This can be a serious barrier for organizational flexibility as well as a factor facilitating such flexibility (Schein, 1992). Although the organizational culture is created, embedded and transmitted to others as a result of internal processes, critical incidents and characteristics of the organization, it is also reflecting the environmental conditions within which the organization finds itself.

Knowledge organizations are usually facing high and rising expectations from customers regarding competence, professionalism and behavioural consistency. The organizational culture can actually contribute to this in the sense that certain perceptions, attitudes and behavioural patterns become legitimized or recommended, whereas other 'pictures of the world' are rejected. This requires, however, that the organizational culture is tuned to the actual demands on the organization, which is often not the case. As the culture is a product of a (for the organization) lifelong moulding process, the culture often tends to be fairly conservative. Organizational defence mechanisms (Argyris, 1990) can prevent organizational members from perceiving objectively strengths and weaknesses of the organization, and thereby often overlooking indications of needs for change.

In organizations with fairly large numbers of professional staff (knowledge workers), a dilemma can occur between the loyalty towards the organization and loyalty towards the professional culture. This is illustrated in Table 7.1.

The organizational citizen is the well-known, loyal employee having internalized to a high extent the organizational culture, defending the company and the current practice. The professional specialist has absorbed a professional culture, usually as a result of university education, and tends to accept organizational demands only to the extent that they do not conflict with his or her professional identity. The alienated employee is

Table 7.1 Commitment to a profession and an organization

| | | Commitment to task or profession | |
		Low	High
Commitment to the organization	Low	The alienated employee	The professional specialist
	High	The organizational citizen	The double-decker

obviously a misfit, usually quite unhappy with the situation and likely to leave the organization (if attractive alternatives exist). The double-decker is managing to give a high level of commitment to the organization and the profession at the same time. This is obviously a very advantageous situation for the organization (and, possibly the employee), but very difficult to establish or maintain in practice.

Organizational flexibility usually does not stem from the organizational citizens. They are so well adjusted to the tasks and cultural assumptions of the organization, that they find it hard to accept attempts to criticize the organization or make it change. The professional specialists may – due to their comprehensive professional background – see a number of potential improvements, but tend to forget the organizational inertia which may block redirection or change attempts. The alienated worker may be very aware of the need for change, but is usually not considered an example to follow. Finally, the double-decker may have high status in the organization, and people will tend to listen to suggestions from him or her. They may be powerful change agents, but are usually few in numbers.

In all, it is difficult to achieve organizational flexibility using organizational culture as the catalyst. The culture will in many cases be more of a barrier than a facilitator for flexibility. However, actual job behaviour and incidents/experiences occurring on the job may contribute to create (provoke) new perceptions about the organization – and hence stimulate flexibility. This is the topic for the following section.

Experiential learning

Performing a job exposes the person to a number of problems, choices and experiences. Acting in a specific situation, observing the consequences of this piece of action and receiving support or sanctions from the environment is a potential learning process (Boak et al., 1991; Mumford, 1982; Pedler, 1991; Stuart, 1984). Some of the problems people are exposed to and some of the actions they engage in are most likely an 'attack' on present routines, norms and attitudes. This constitutes potentially an experiential learning process resulting from the actual performance on the job, rather than participation in formalized training activities (Revans, 1982).

The middle manager plays a crucial role in this (London, 1988; Margerison, 1987). First, the manager is usually heavily involved in the (re)design of jobs in his or her own unit, and job design means designing (or removing) potential learning opportunities for/from subordinates. Second, the human resource responsibility of the manager implies that the manager should be interested in ways of satisfying training needs – among which is experiential learning. Third, the manager plays a key role in enacting the 'rules' of interacting with the environment and, hence, approves/disapproves certain experiential learning situations.

This perception has several consequences. First, in order to stimulate the development of skills, one has to look at the learning potential of the specific job and redesign it accordingly. Second, not only the job situation but a number of off-the-job activities possess a learning potential which can spill over on the job. Examples of this are political work, sports, charity work, etc. Third, the development of managerial skills cannot be monitored and controlled to the same extent as a mechanistic management training programme. This is particularly evident in the case of achieving managerial skills.

However, one should be cautious of the many potential individual barriers for experiential learning. First, 'incomplete learning cycles' (March and Olsen, 1976) can prevent one from learning, or from learning the right thing, from performing a task. Also, there are other blockages for the transformation of human action into experiences. Finally, even if experiences do occur, you might not draw the right conclusions – and hence learn the right thing – from these experiences.

Also, the job itself can block the creation of learning experiences. The entire field of job design (Hackman and Oldham, 1980, Stewart, 1982) is giving convincing evidence that the routinization of, or perception of demands/constraints in, a given job can be a serious barrier for the creation of a demanding and challenging job situation.

Finally, one often finds organizational barriers which can prevent or reduce learning (Pfeffer, 1994). The defence mechanisms of organizations (Argyris, 1990) can be so strong that one has to create 'minor explosions' or deliberate friction to create a space for organizational learning. Bushe and Shani even suggest 'parallel learning structures', by which they understand 'interventions where (a) a "structure" (...) is created that (b) operates "parallel" ... with the formal hierarchy and structure and (c) has the purpose of increasing an organization's "learning"' (Bushe and Shani, 1991: 9).

However, the existence and the awareness of these organizational barriers should not lead to giving up on aspirations of intensifying learning and change processes – with the aim of enhancing organizational flexibility. On the contrary, they should lead to the construction of an intervention strategy incorporating these organizational defence mechanisms. This eventually provides the prerequisites for a comprehensive organizational change process, equivalent with what, to an increasing extent, is called organizational learning.

There is still much controversy over the concept of organizational learning. In particular, it is debatable whether learning at an organizational level can actually be distinguished from individual learning (Redding and Catalanello, 1994). Despite the very blurred picture, however, a learning-intensive environment (whether it is at the organizational or individual level) will most often stimulate flexibility. The middle managers play a vital role in this as their key position in the organization can block organizational change and personal development at the same time (Johnson and Frohman, 1989). Alternatively, middle managers can function as 'change agents' and thereby facilitate the organization change process (London, 1988).

In the next section, we look in particular at the HR role of the middle manager.

Human resource management responsibility

The integration of business strategy and HRM strategy is influencing, and being influenced by, the location of HRM responsibility and tasks in the organization. As mentioned above, the business strategy, usually determined at the top organizational level, is subdivided and operationalized as it is transmitted through the organization. Not surprisingly, then, decentralization is usually followed by assignment of HRM responsibility to line (including middle) managers (Stähle and Schirmer, 1992). This has a strong impact on the division of labour between the line manager and the HR manager:

Responsibility for personnel management/HRM is increasingly integrated into the line management of decentralized operations, which proponents of HRM advocate. Guest (1987, p. 51) for example, suggests that 'if HRM is to be taken seriously, personnel managers must give it away'. But when those personnel managers give it away in the decentralized organization, they may also give it up.

(Blyton and Turnbull, 1992: 11)

Each organizational entity is made responsible for achieving certain organizational objectives by pursuing a specific business strategy. As human resources are the predominant production factor in knowledge organizations, an HR strategy becomes vital for the realization of the business strategy. This emphasis on decentralized HRM responsibility does not preclude that the top management forum attributes increasing importance to the HR area. In fact, the two trends go well hand in hand.

In this chapter, assignment of HRM responsibility is defined as 'the degree to which HRM practice involves and gives responsibility to line managers rather than personnel specialists' (Brewster and Larsen, 1993).[1] There is an increasing recognition of this issue in the literature (see, for example, Brewster and Connock 1985; Freedman, 1991; Schuler, 1990; Torrington, 1989; Watson, 1989). With the closer link between strategy development and human resource development, it is anticipated that middle managers will be given a primary responsibility for HRM. It is argued that within the major areas of HRM (attracting, retaining, motivating and developing staff) the middle manager needs to be aware of the synergy between human, financial and physical resources. For him or her, allocating time, money and energy to the development of subordinate staff is an investment in enhanced effectiveness and future success; and there is no way this responsibility can be picked up by the human resource manager. The HRM function is seen as playing the role of co-ordinator and catalyst for the activities of line managers – a 'management team player ... working (jointly) with the line manager solving people-related business issues' (Schuler, 1990: 51).

Assignment of HR responsibilities to line managers is driven by both organizational and effectiveness criteria. Organizationally, it is now widely believed that the responsibility for human resources should be located where decisions about the allocation of all resources (including human resources) are assigned, in order to meet the objectives of the organization – in practice, as we shall show, that increasingly means with line management rather than specialist functions. For most organizations the most expensive item of operating costs is the employees. Hence, in cost or profit-centre based organizations (in the private or public sectors), there is pressure to include management of human resource in line management responsibilities.

Effectively, it is only by motivating and committing the workforce that value can be added to other resources. It is line managers, not specialist staff functions, who are in frequent, often constant, contact with employees. For most employees it is their immediate superiors who represent the management of the company. Furthermore, it is line managers, rather than HR specialists, who have the information needed to assess employees' competence and their needs for further training and development. This is particularly the case at the middle management level.

THREE CASE STUDIES

In this section, we will present three case studies which illustrate the (changing) roles of middle managers. All three cases are Danish: a governmental agency, a hi-tech manufacturing company and a partly privatized state institution. The structure of each case study is the same. First, the organization is presented. Second, the specific change activities are described. Finally, the change processes are analysed from a double perspective: a middle manager view and a national (Danish) culture perspective.

The Ministry of Education

Introduction

This case describes a management development programme in a major governmental agency (Head et al., 1993; Larsen, 1993). The emphasis is put on the managerial role of the participants, the learning methodology as well as the outcome of the programme.

The ministry has the overall responsibility for the educational activities taking place in primary and secondary schools, vocational schools, universities and other related institutions. This sector employs in total approximately 150,000 people. At the time of this programme (1987–88), the administrative core of the ministry had about 800 employees. It was organized into nine divisions, each headed by a division head (deputy permanent secretary).

The ministry had a bureaucratic culture with a high emphasis on the 'written word', coupled with a strong belief in harmony. Unlike most other bureaucratic organizations, the ministry was characterized by informal interpersonal behaviour, low power distance and a humanistic atmosphere.

The management development programme

The programme had three central objectives. The first was to enable the organization to cope with an ever-increasing workload at the same time as there was a cut in staff. The second was to improve the ministry's ability to adapt quickly to rapidly changing external demands. The third was to stimulate (an understanding of) professional management. Managerial staff had mainly been playing the role of specialists, monitoring the technical quality of the work of others, rather than focusing on managerial tasks. Also, the human resource responsibility of line managers for subordinates was poorly developed.

Once it had been decided to initiate the programme, a major decision was the definition of the target group. The ministry and the external consultants hired to conduct the actual programme agreed on selecting all those persons who had a real, genuine impact on managerial processes, rather than looking solely on whether people possessed a formal managerial position in the organization. However, this organic selection criterion turned out to be so difficult to apply that the actual group of participants became the top fifty-four managers of the organization. Approximately ten of these constituted the top management team, whereas the remaining part (and hence the majority) were middle managers. It was never stated explicitly that the programme was compulsory, but the common understanding was that all managers had to participate and nobody seemed to object to this.

114

Strong emphasis was put on informing (managerial and non-managerial) staff about the programme prior to the actual start. There was a very positive reaction by non-managerial staff to the fact that the programme was not a manager development programme, aimed at developing fifty-four individuals, but rather a comprehensive management development programme.

In order to diagnose the organizational 'reality' and establish close links with the client, the consultants did three things. First, they conducted individual or group interviews with approximately 150 persons in the organization. All fifty-four participants were interviewed individually, and some 100 non-managerial staff (selected by and among the non-managerial staff) were interviewed individually or in groups. In addition, the consultants attended and observed a number of regular staff meetings in the organization, including the weekly management briefing with the Minister of Education. Third, a reference group was established as a central forum for contact between the consultants and the client. The members of the reference group were eight representatives of the participants, the Permanent Secretary and the team of consultants. Also, the principal spokeswoman of the non-managerial staff was a member of the group even though she did not participate in the programme as such.

The interview phase provided unique data about management and human resource problems of the organization and served as raw material for a working paper, giving an 'X-ray' of the organization. This paper, which was written by the consultants, did not interpret or evaluate the situation, but described and summarized the situation as it had been expressed through the interviews. In this way it would be up to the organization to decide what to do about the problems expressed in the paper. The paper was distributed to all staff and was intensively discussed in the organization – informally and formally. Thus, it was discussed at seminars with representatives of all staff groups. Also, the top management team had a twenty-four hour workshop during which the team defined ten areas which would be given high priority in the future. These ten areas of action were communicated to and discussed with the organization, revised and eventually reconfirmed by the top management team. One of these areas of priority was the human resource responsibility of line managers.

The activities described so far (the information phase, the interview procedure and the diagnostic working paper) were not just an initial start or diagnosis of the change process. On the contrary, they were an important first step of the change process itself. Of great impact was that a very large part of the entire organization was *de facto* involved in diagnosing the actual situation and/or discussing potential strategies for implementing change in the organization.

The formal learning activities of the programme consisted of two mainstreams: management courses and individual projects. The courses covered managerial issues with strong emphasis on the problems discovered during the initial interview study. The content of the courses was not developed until after the diagnosis. Emphasis was placed on 'down-to-earth' subjects and experiential exercises, rather than abstract conceptualization of general management problems.

Immediately after the first course module, each participant was asked to define a personal management project theme, which: (1) contained important, complex management problems of a specific, realistic nature, (2) was of personal interest to the participant, (3) was of importance to the organization, (4) involved some degree of risk taking, (5) necessitated joint effort by the participant and his or her subordinates in order to be solved, (6) had a clear formulation of the targeted end result, and (7) could be documented and evaluated.

This design reflected an experiential learning model, according to which learning is facilitated if people are placed in an experience-loaded environment, involving a certain degree of risk-taking and with a high level of commitment to the task performed. Also, as with the general programme, it was believed that management was not (solely) the behaviour, style or attitude of a specific group of individuals (managers). Management was rather viewed as an interpersonal process of influence and power. Therefore it was important to include the subordinates in the project work, although they did not take part in the courses.

The participants could choose a task (project theme) which was known or new to them. They could solve this problem by a known or a new method, and do it in co-operation with well-known or new persons/organizations. However, it was not allowed to 'play safe' on all three dimensions, as this would restrict the learning potential of the project. Neither was it recommended to 'throw oneself at the deep end', as the risk-taking on all three dimensions would be too demanding. Thus, it was recommended to experiment on one or two dimensions.

The project proposals had to be presented in writing and accepted by the top management team and the consultants. In the course of the project work, progress reports had to be produced at regular intervals. The consultants played the role of being process consultants, in that one consultant was linked to each project. The projects had to be finished in eight months which was coinciding with the official termination of the programme as a whole. At that time, a residential two-day seminar was held to present the results of the project work, evaluate the programme as a whole and decide on follow-up activities of the programme.

The evaluation of the management development programme showed that the initial reception of the programme was quite positive, even among non-managerial staff who did not show symptoms of jealousy. The organization was quite excited by the diagnostic interviews, and the working paper was received with curiosity and excitement. The training courses were considered to be reasonable.

The individual projects were generally considered to be interesting, necessary and important, but also time-consuming. An attempt by the consultants to form small groups of participants who could support each other with the project work was rejected by the organization due to the workload already involved in the programme. The motivation and energy, with which the programme participants dealt with their projects, varied greatly.

An overall evaluation of the results of the programme and its consequences was effected at an evaluation seminar four months after the formal end of the programme. About fifty persons participated in this seminar, including the top management team, representatives of participants and their subordinate staff, the reference group and the consultants. The seminar report indicates that the top management team had enhanced its consciousness about and ability to carry out its strategic management role. The team had become more visible and significant in the organization. At the same time the meetings of the team had become more frank resulting in more fruitful discussions. The management group as a whole (the fifty-four participants) had for the first time been together and participated in a common long-lasting process. The programme had clearly led to an increased consciousness of the managers' roles, tasks and possibilities.

In the area of human resources management both managers and their staff had become much more aware of the content and importance of the staff development role of line managers. Despite this, only few specific improvements were achieved in this area.

In general, there was a great variation of opinion as to whether management functions were better executed than before, dependent on the persons and subject areas concerned. The individual development projects clearly carried a central part of the effect of the project. Roughly estimated, a third of the projects had a rather significant effect, another third had a positive effect, although not overwhelming. The last third of the projects either didn't find new paths or never started. However, it should be kept in mind that in total more than fifty projects were running at the same time. This contributed to developing a climate of development and renewal, even though some projects were very poor.

Despite these positive results, there were limits to the effect of the programme. The general bureaucratic culture with its intellectual and analytical approach to change persevered and acted so as to curb the action orientation which began to emerge. Also, the traditional culture counteracted a more extrovert orientation towards the 'customers' of the ministry.

Although we have focused exclusively on the management development programme, it should be mentioned that a large number of other development processes took place at the same time or in the following years. The ministry underwent an information technology 'revolution', a design programme, an effectiveness programme and a change in organizational structure. A development dialogue programme (that is, annual performance talks) was introduced, and this was later hooked on to a vision management programme. The idea of this programme was to discuss the overall visions and objectives of the organization and relate these to the 'psychological contract' of each individual.

The vision reports were written by a central planning function of the organization, but based on close interaction with all layers of the organization. The middle managers were attributed a vital role as 'ambassadors' for this strategic plan, as well as collectors of input from non-managerial staff and passers of this information to the top management.

In order to match the human resources with the strategic plans, a comprehensive employee development programme was initiated. All staff were given an almost free choice of a series of courses as well as on-the-job learning activities. The idea was that all development activities should facilitate the synergy between individual and organizational development. Thus, the range of development activities were designed in such a way that it stimulated the development of skills needed for the implementation of the vision reports. Also, the annual performance dialogues were extended with a couple of questions dealing with the individual consequences for the person in question of the organizational vision and objectives.

Discussion

The case illustrates how the very precise perception by the organization of the crucial role of its middle managers initiated the management development programme. Delimiting the target group for this programme showed how difficult it is to define managerial roles and behaviours in an organization.

The case also shows the consequences of a process-oriented management development programme (rather than an individualized manager development programme). First, the focus (and change facilitator) was the management processes, rather than individual behaviour of present or potential managers. Second, the organization avoided the potential element of self-fulfilling prophecies and organizational jealousy which can be the byproduct of an élitist identification of a small group of 'high-fliers'. However, the organization did not succeed in selecting the participants on the basis of a non-dogmatic assessment of their involvement in managerial processes, rather than formal positions. Instead, hierarchical position was used as a selection criterion.

The formal training activities of the management development programme created a concentrated and often undisturbed learning environment. The rationally developed course programme and methods catered to the specific needs of the participants and facilitated a certain amount of experimentation in a protected environment.

However, the main focus in the programme was on experiential learning situations. The advantages of these were more realistic learning tasks and more authentic outcomes, easier implementation of the learning outcome, a training content finely tuned to the actual demands of the organization. Also experiential learning was more cost-effective than formal training.

The middle managers were clearly given the role of strategic ambassador, change agent and cultural catalyst. The subsequent vision management programme – supported by the staff development programme and the revision of the performance talks – reinforced the role of the middle manager as a strategic link between top management and the non-managerial staff. However, the case study also shows that the considerable improvement of organizational effectiveness achieved was due to a number of initiatives. In reality, the effect of the management development programme is confounded with other intervention strategies.

When the management development programme was designed and carried through, it was not considered whether the programme reflected specific Danish national culture characteristics. However, a subsequent *ex post facto* analysis (in co-operation with US researchers) has detected that the programme does actually have a 'Danish Design' flavour. This is illustrated by referring to the cultural mapping of Hofstede (1980, 1991), based on the four variables:

- feminity vs. masculinity
- individualism vs. collectivism
- power distance
- uncertainty avoidance.

Hofstede's cultural dimensions will also be used to discuss the two other cases. However, for a more detailed presentation of Hofstede's general findings, reference is made to his original works (see above).

The Danish national culture is in Hofstede's study feminine in nature. This is reflected in the management development programme in a number of ways. Great emphasis was placed on interpersonal processes, social skills, consensus and suppression of conflict. Also, the selection criteria for the participants initially did not include hierarchical level, and various attempts were made to include people who did participate informally in managerial processes. As mentioned above, this criterion eventually had to be abandoned.

Moderate individualism is another characteristic feature of the Danish national culture. Rather than putting high-fliers of the organization on the fast track, this management development process removed the distinction between individual development, management development and organization development.

The project work reinforced the link between the participant and his or her subordinates, but was also seen as a catalyst for organizational change. Great emphasis was placed on strengthening the competence of the group of participants as a whole, rather than explicating the progress of the individual members.

In Hofstede's study, the Danish national score for power distance is very low. The fact that non-managerial staff were not only interviewed as part of the diagnosis procedure, but also received the resulting working paper and were involved in determining appropriate course of action as a consequence of the working paper, shows how the distance between organizational levels is modest.

The fourth cultural dimension is uncertainty avoidance. Although the programme as a whole was fairly structured, a lot of ambiguity and uncertainty was deliberately built into the programme. Hence, the content of the course modules was not determined in advance. Participants were encouraged to experiment in their project work and go for the good learning experience, rather than the 'right solution' to the task in question, if unable to achieve both objectives. The heavy process (rather than outcome) orientation of the programme as such put focus on 'how we are moving', rather than 'where we are going'.

In short, despite the fact that neither the client nor the team of (Danish) consultants were aware of the particular national 'flavour' of the management development programme, this cultural bias was evident – and visible when seen from the outside.

Oticon

Introduction

Oticon is a hearing aids manufacturing company which made a dramatic turn-round in the early 1990s (Peters, 1992; Poulsen,

1993). The company was established almost ninety years ago, has approximately 1,600 employees and is the world's third largest producer of hearing aids. Although the company was very successful in the past and eventually achieved a position as one of the world's leading suppliers, through the 1980s it faced increasing financial and organizational problems. In fact, the organization had all the strengths and weaknesses of traditional, hierarchical organizations including formal procedures, a conservative culture, employee loyalty and consensus-seeking (or conflict-avoiding) behaviour. The organization failed to adjust to the rapidly changing market conditions. These problems escalated to the point where it was obvious that radical steps had to be taken. The first step was the recruitment of a new chief executive officer in 1988, who was given full responsibility for implementing the necessary changes in the organization.

'Think the unthinkable'

Rather than initiating a long series of minor, incremental changes, the newly appointed CEO suggested a very broad package of innovative and radical initiatives in organizational structure, job design, information technology and physical layout of the company. All these steps of action were contained in a memo, 'Think the unthinkable', which was written by the new CEO and distributed to all staff in early 1990. The suggested changes were:

- replacing a hierarchical job structure with a project-based organization where each employee is involved in a number of (often cross-organizational and cross-functional) projects at the same time, and where each project is considered as a 'business unit' with its own resources, time schedule and success criteria
- abandoning traditional managerial jobs and attributing managerial authority to the project groups or the individual employee
- stimulating informal oral communication by establishing coffee bars and meeting facilities in the office building
- reducing drastically written paper communication by establishing electronic scanning of all incoming mail as well as very comprehensive IT systems, networks, etc.

122

- facilitating physical mobility by creating an open space office where each person has a cart or trolley (that is, a desk on wheels) containing their computer, phone and a limited space for paper.

The overall objective of this – which was stated explicitly in the paper – was increasing effectiveness by 30 per cent in three years.

The plan was implemented in 1991 when the headquarters was relocated to a building which had been especially designed to maximize the physical flexibility. Hence, a large open space office made the free movement of the trolleys possible, and the coffee bars, the canteen and the wide stairway created extensive opportunities for informal exchange of information and experiences.

A number of symbolic acts and psychological elements supported the change process:

- The CEO stressed clearly and frequently that most of his ideas about managing an organization came from the boy scout movement which he was, and had for a long time been, involved in.
- All incoming mail is delivered to one particular room where the employees come to read it. All important mail is scanned into the electronic information system, after which the paper is shredded. The paper-shredder is connected to a transparent tube which passes right through the canteen. The symbolic effect of seeing all the shredded paper is quite noticeable.
- The CEO has stated publicly that he, when taking over his position, also bought a fairly large portion of the company's shares (and had to raise a bank loan to do this). By stressing this he has made it evident to the employees that his own financial security is at great risk if the company does not succeed.
- His entire managerial style which is very much characterized by openness, dialogue, informality, experimentation and humbleness has to a large extent influenced the culture and value system of the organization.

In short, the development of the organization can be described in the following way:

- from hierarchy to project organization
- from formal information to informal dialogue

- from managerial positions to leadership processes
- from .departmentalization to cross-functional thinking and working
- from written communication to electronic networks
- from supervisory control to control of self
- from extrinsic rewards to intrinsic motivation.

Discussion

The very comprehensive and radical change process which the organization went through supports the stereotyped perception that in the future middle managers will be fewer in numbers and significance. Whereas the old organization had a very top-heavy authority system and a 'full team' of middle managers, there are hardly any middle managers left, as the company is turned into a project-based organization.

Top management decides which projects should be started up and who should be the project manager, but the project managers have got the proper responsibility for resources, outcome, budget and timetable for their own project. A few senior specialists (mainly middle managers from the 'old' organization) have a technical, semi-managerial position. Otherwise, it is a two-layered organization where titles and job descriptions have been abandoned. In principle, all employees can become project managers, and the project manager for one project will be subordinated to other project managers in the other projects.

The human resource responsibility is undertaken collectively by the group of project managers, for whom a given employee works at any given time. This is not an ideal situation and much effort is being invested in finding better ways to ensure a proper undertaking of the responsibility for human resources. A system of decentralized 'personnel managers' which was suggested in the original 'manifest' of the CEO, was never implemented as it would restrict the managerial informality and flexibility.

A critical question is the degree of uniqueness of this case. The change process in itself is almost unique, but the background, that is, the company situation prior to the turn-round, is very typical for many historically successful companies. There were no significant factors which conditioned (and made possible) the change process. The fact that in the past the company was financially successful can impede the organizational alertness, 'fighter' spirit and the realistic recognition of the need for increased productivity. The organization became self-sufficient, and external (or internal) indications of 'something going wrong' were projected, rejected or ridiculed.

Another critical question is the role of the CEO. The unique combination of creativity, courage, informality, respect for others, egalitarianism and humour, which characterizes the CEO, has been an important facilitator for the change process. The CEO has been very visible in the process, and media coverage frequently tends to make him the hero or even solely responsible for the success of the turn-round. However, this visibility is in contrast to the intensity with which the CEO has, constantly, stressed (and shown in his own behaviour) that there have been 1,600 heroes, and that he has only invented the general framework and, after that, been the symbolic representation and personification of the change process.

A third critical question relates to the attitudes of the employees to the turn-round. If the employees had not known it before, they certainly realized by the very arrival of the new CEO, how counter-productive development had been through the 1980s. The authoritarian leadership style, the indirect communication, the exaggerated loyalty and respect, combined with a profound belief that this was nevertheless a successful company, was a dangerous cocktail. The initial stages of the turn-around created anxiety and fear, but the honest, open and informal behaviour of the CEO eventually reduced this anxiety. Also, due to the intensive media coverage of the experiment, the employees gradually considered themselves as being very fortunate, interesting and progressive. How could one complain about a company which is catching global interest and turns up on BBC, CNN, etc.?

A fourth issue is whether the case is so embedded in the Danish culture that it could not take place in other national cultures. Studies of national culture characteristics (in particular the work done by Hofstede (1980, 1991)) indicates that the Danish national culture is characterized by moderate individualism, femininity, small distance of power and low uncertainty avoidance. In a sense, this makes Denmark an ideal setting for a case like Oticon. The entire set-up for the organization change process reflects this national culture profile. However, one should keep in mind that Oticon prior to 1988 did have an entirely different profile still, residing within the same national culture.

The Danish Patent Office

Introduction

The Danish Patent Office (DPO) is a governmental agency ensuring the industrial property rights of companies by issuing patents and registering trade marks, utility models, designs and chips (Sinding et al., 1994). Up until the early 1980s, the organization was very traditional and old-fashioned. So, although its domain is dealing with the latest inventions in business, it was in itself a very non-progressive organization.

In 1983, the strategic position of the DPO was very difficult. For a number of years, the Danish Government had postponed the decision of whether Denmark should accede the so-called European Patent Convention (EPC). This agreement implies that applications can be filed directly at the central European Patent Office, thus reducing dramatically the need for a proper Danish Patent Office. This explains why the Government for a number of years had been very reluctant to allocate resources (mainly manpower) to the DPO. However, this meant that applications were piling up in the DPO and the waiting time for having applications dealt with also went up. This not only created frustration among customers, but threatened the protection of the subject of application, for example, inventions.

Semi-autonomous groups

As the Government (in 1983) for the third time refrained from acceding the convention, it was decided to allocate more manpower to the organization, under the condition that the organization became more effective. Consequently, a major organization development programme was initiated. It included a vast number of interviews, seminars and communication activities and created an awareness about the present situation as well as a commitment to change this. Eventually, it was decided to turn the part of the organization dealing with applications into a number of semi-autonomous groups (sections). It was up to each individual section to choose its own management model, but all groups went for collective management, and were hence sharing the managerial duties rather than having one person managing the group. Some of the previous section heads were given senior specialist jobs in the new groups and others decided to leave, as they didn't believe in the new system.

Obviously, although the autonomous group structure implied a drastic reduction in the number of middle managers, it did not make superfluous the need for co-ordination and monitoring of the groups. Hence, a system of consultants and co-ordinators was established in the organization. The consultants were providing professional technical support in complex matters and thereby securing the quality of the work done. The co-ordinators were securing the performance, that is, the quantity of the performance of the groups.

The organization developed further, and many development initiatives were launched, including radical changes in the IT systems as well as the introduction of a dialogue-based performance appraisal system. Also, the DPO obtained status as a government enterprise, meaning that the domain of competence of the DPO increased, provided that the organization made a certain minimum profit every year. Finally, the DPO relocated to a new and bigger building with better storage facilities for the 25 million applications. This physical relocation away from an old, dark and dusty building in itself gave a 'kick' to organizational life.

A significant event was the accession to the European Patent Convention, which came into effect in 1990. Like in the early 1980s, the DPO was now at a strategic crossroad. Should the DPO be reduced to a mailbox, forwarding the applications to the European Patent Office, or should it enlarge its area of business and become a technological knowledge and service centre for Danish companies? A major market research project was initiated and the result of this was a clear recommendation of turning the DPO into such a knowledge and service centre for Danish enterprises.

Unfortunately, it still took a while before the Government was convinced that it would be wise to allocate more resources to the DPO, to make the organization more visible to the business community, and to market knowledge services based on the patent library, database networks and professional expertise of the DPO. In the meantime, the level of frustration in the organization increased significantly. The performance decreased, some of the autonomous sections did not undertake their managerial responsibility, and there was an increasing scepticism towards the managerial and organizational structure as a whole.

Back to middle managers

In 1991, an action-learning based management development programme was started. As there were only very few appointed managers in the organization, the programme was open for anybody who was capable of and interested in taking part in managerial processes. It was very deliberate that the target group did not only consist of appointed and/or potential managers as a fairly large part of the organization did not have any managers and there was a strong belief in collective leadership. There were managerial processes all over the place, however, and in order to professionalize these, the management development programme was initiated.

Also, it was decided to undertake an organizational survey which was named 'OD 92'. Surprising to most groups in the organization, there was a widespread dissatisfaction with the collective management form. Hence, top management decided, after they had discussed the issue with staff representatives, to abandon the collective management form and appoint formal managers for all sections. The managers were all recruited internally, but had to go through a comprehensive selection procedure, encompassing psychological testing by an external consulting firm. Shortly after this, the performance appraisal system was supplemented by a mutual assessment procedure between managers and their subordinates. Also, a performance-based compensation system was introduced. These various initiatives all reflected a move towards a more 'hard-nosed' business environment with emphasis on measuring performance, providing feedback and individualizing the work environment (a large contrast to the previously dominant collective and egalitarian culture).

Discussion

This case study shows an organization which in the first wave changed identity from being low-key, invisible and reactive to being more outspoken, aggressive and progressive in terms of managerial practice (that is, the autonomous work groups), but which in the second phase tightened up the organization, reintroduced appointed managers, established comprehensive performance measuring schemes and became customer oriented, knowledge based and visible. This all happened in a decade and had considerable consequences for the middle manager role. In the initial period, managers were mostly appointed on the basis of their professional (functional) qualifications (mainly as engineers or lawyers). In the second phase, the organization had removed most middle managers, replacing them by collective leadership. In the third phase, the middle managers were reintroduced, appointed on the basis of their managerial skills and with widespread managerial power. As it appears, this case is an illustration of the fact that organizational change processes might mean a decrease in the number and significance of middle managers. However, this does not preclude the very same organization at a later stage from re-establishing a 'thick' middle management level.

An interesting issue is how the organization 'was surprised' by finding out that the general opinion was against the autonomous work groups. An answer to this is that the autonomous work group concept was so unique that it became part of the identity and image of the organization. The (moderate level of) daily annoyance and critique of organizational processes never questioned the underlying group concept as such – only the way it was functioning. Although it was not quite taboo to state that the autonomous groups should be abandoned, it was rarely done. In fact, the dual ladder system with co-ordinators and consultants was blamed for communication difficulties, clashing interests and suboptimization.

Although the organization was (and is) characterized by a high level of 'freedom of speech' and respect for the individual, an anonymous survey was the vehicle for the detection of organizational rhetorics. The survey data made it legitimate to discuss alternatives to the 'best of all worlds'.

A second critical question is what could have caused the autonomous group structure to survive, rather than being replaced by a hierarchical structure. An important answer is that the group concept was in itself sound, and the organization had managed to introduce systems (like management development, annual development talks, etc.) which would normally require

129

a structure with managerial positions. Hence, the strength of the group structure was considerable, which partly explains the fact that the group structure 'survived' for a number of years.

If some of the perceived weaknesses and problems had been dealt with, the group structure possibly could have been sustained. However, these problems were probably not discussed enough in the organization, and attributed to other causes anyway. Also, the societal development at the same time stressed values like individualization, performance management, emphasis on managerial skills, psychological testing, etc.

Appointing managers for all sections brought the organization back to mainstream organization design. As most stakeholders agreed that this would be the right thing to do, it can be considered as a step forward. However, the autonomous group model provided extraordinary learning possibilities, empowerment and employee involvement in managerial processes. This got lost, and as a result of this, the organization lost an importance competence-building device. As it appears from the case description, the organization has, since the displacement of the autonomous groups, started up a number of development activities. Hence, the organization may actually (today) be more of a learning organization than before, but this is in spite of the displacement of the groups, not because of it.

A third issue is how an organization can become less dependent on external circumstances (as in the Government's decision (not) to accede the European Patent Convention). Traditionally, organizations are adapting to external circumstances. As it were, the DPO had only a few degrees of freedom in the situation where the Government could not 'make up its mind', apart from negotiations with the Ministry of Industry and usual lobbying activities. However, the long-term survival was mainly caused by the fact that the overall objectives and role of the organization were redefined. It is to an increasing extent considered being part of strategic management to inverse the causal relationship and make the organization have an impact on the environment. The DPO survived because it possessed a high degree of functional flexibility and had been able to make visible to society that the organization could turn into a knowledge and service centre for the business community.

Analysing the case from a national (Danish) culture perspective is a complex issue. The introduction of the semi-autonomous sections, the strategy seminars and the management development programme initiated in the mid and late 1980s, respectively, can be interpreted as 'typical' for a low power distance, low uncertainty avoidance, feminist culture. The democratic structure, the influence given to non-managerial staff and the non-élitist approach to management development fits into Hofstede's profile of the Danish culture. What explains, then, how the pendulum swung back to the other extremity, when managers were reintroduced in 1992? One possible explanation is the general trend in the Danish society in the late 1980s and early 1990s, emphasizing values such as performance, accountability, individualization and liability. This change in value orientation which coincided with a movement to the right in Danish politics and a bad national economy, led to an interest in individualizing performance, success and failure. A hierarchical managerial structure facilitated this.

Another possible explanation may be that the organization 'outlived' the democratic structure. Despite all their virtues (and the positive image they created), the autonomous sections had their weaknesses. So, although the organization was very tuned in to exchange of ideas, opinions and feedback, the autonomous sections became a 'mantra' and could not easily be challenged.

Thirdly, as pointed out by Sinding et al., the organization was very flexible:

> This made possible the introduction of AWGs (autonomous work groups) in the first place, but also increased the ability and desire to handle organizational changes afterwards. Hence, the O.D.[organizational development] change in 1983 in itself improved the ability of the organization to make another (later) O.D. change, neutralizing the first one! (Sinding et al., 1994: 83).

CONCLUSION

The three case studies show very different roles of line managers. In the Ministry of Education, middle managers were used as means of increasing effectiveness, strategic orientation and flexibility of the organization. At Oticon, the very comprehensive and multi-area turn-round (almost) implied the abandonment of middle managers. The Patent Office also (initially) removed middle managers, but reintroduced them after eight years of an autonomous group structure.

The three cases have, in different ways and to different degrees, supported the hypothesis that middle managers play four key roles:

- an integrative role as a strategic link
- a facilitator (or barrier) for cultural flexibility
- an agent for experiential learning processes embedded in the job context
- a location for human resource responsibility.

The confirmation of this hypothesis does not say anything about the generalizability of these results. The cases may be very atypical and can hence not be generalized. However, Jaeger (1986) has put forward a hypothesis that Danish culture is very compatible with the underlying values of organization development. He bases this hypothesis on an analysis of Hofstede's cultural dimensions as they relate to the theory of OD as well as the various national cultures. Jaeger's conclusion is interesting as OD as a discipline was invented in the US, where cultural profile (according to Jaeger) deviates from the ideal OD culture characteristics. The three cases certainly illustrate how organizations with low power distance and low uncertainty avoidance can initiate non-élitist management development programmes, relying heavily on (and experimenting with) experiential learning processes and with an underlying notion of management being intersubjective processes of influence, rather than individual behaviour or attitudes of identified managerial staff.

The conclusion of this chapter is that the complexity regarding middle managers in general is certainly not any less when dealing with knowledge organizations. This type of organization at the same time stresses the need for middle managers and provides examples of situations where middle managers are superfluous. Situational factors as well as specific characteristics of the organization in question (including its culture, industry, etc.) determine what appropriate middle management is. The three case studies have provided three different illustrations of this.

NOTES

1 It is very difficult to find a word which does not necessarily imply that the HRM responsibility has been *moved* from the centre to the individual line manager. We have previously (Brewster and Larsen, 1992) used the term 'devolvement' with the undesired connotation that the HRM responsibility is 'handed over' to somebody. Hence, we have in the present chapter chosen the more neutral word 'assignment' which rather indicates the actual *location* of HRM responsibility.

REFERENCES

Argyris, C. (1990) *Overcoming Organizational Defenses. Facilitating Organizational Learning*, Boston: Allyn and Bacon.

Blyton, P. and Turnbull, P. (1992) *Reassessing Human Resource Management*, London: Sage.

Boak, G., Thompson, D. and Mitchell, L. (1991) *Developing Managerial Competences. The Management Learning Contract Approach*, London: Pitman.

Borucki, C., Byosier, P.H.R. and Dopson, S. (1992) 'Changes in the role of middle management. A European view', Proceedings of the Third Conference on International Personnel and Human Resources Management, Ashridge Management College, 2–4 July.

Brewster, C. and Connock, S. (1985) *Industrial Relations: Cost-Effective Strategies*, London: Hutchinson.

Brewster, C. and Larsen, H.H. (1992) 'Human resource management in Europe: evidence from ten countries', *International Journal of Human Resource Management* 3(3): 409–34.

— (1993) 'Human resource management in twelve European countries', Paper presented at the Academy of Management Annual Meeting, Atlanta, GA, 9–11 August.

Bushe, G.R. and Shani, A.B. (1991) *Parallel Learning Structures*, Reading, MA: Addison-Wesley.

Dopson, S., Risk, A. and Stewart, R. (1992) 'The changing role of the middle manager in the United Kingdom', *International Studies of Management and Organization* 22(1): 40–54.

Dopson, S. and Stewart, R. (1990) 'What is happening to middle management', *British Journal of Management* 1: 3–16.

Freedman A. (1991) *The Changing Human Resources Function*, New York: The Conference Board.

Furnham, A. and Gunter, B. (1993) *Corporate Assessment*, London: Routledge.

Guest, D. (1987) 'Human resource management and industrial relations', *Journal of Management Studies* 24(5).

Hackman, J.R. and Oldham, G.R. (1980) *Work Redesign*. Reading, MA: Addison-Wesley.

Hartle, F. (1992) 'Performance management – where is it going?', in,

A. Mitrani, M. Dalziel and D. Fitt *Competency Based Human Resource Management*, London: Kogan Page.

Head, T.C., Larsen, H.H., Nielsen, P.L. and Sørensen, P.F. Jr. (1993) 'The impact of national culture on organizational change: a Danish case study', *International Journal of Public Administration* **16**(11): 1793–1814.

Hofstede, G. (1980) *Culture's Consequences*, Newbury Park, CA: Sage.

— (1991) *Culture and Organizations: Software of the Mind*, London: McGraw-Hill.

Jaeger, A.M. (1986) 'Organization development and national culture: Where is the fit?', *Academy of Management Review* **11**(1): 178–90.

Johnson, L.W. and Frohman, A.L. (1989) 'Identifying and closing the gap in the middle of organizations', *Academy of Management Executive* **3**(2): 107–14.

Larsen, H.H. (1993) *Experiential Learning in Management Development – a Danish Case Study*. Papers in Organization, nr. 10, Institute of Organization and Industrial Sociology.

London, M. (1988) *Change Agents*, San Francisco: Jossey-Bass.

March, J.G. and Olsen, J.P. (1976) *Ambiguity and Choice in Organizations*, Oslo: Universitetsforlaget.

Margerison, C. (1987) 'How to avoid failure and gain success in management development', *Leadership and Organization Development Journal* (UK) **8**(4): 73–86.

Mumford, A.C. (1982) 'Learning style and learning skills', *Journal of Management Development* **1**(2): 55–65.

Nonaka, I. (1991) 'The knowledge-creating company', *Harvard Business Review*, November–December: 96–104.

Pedler, M. (ed.) (1991) *Action Learning in Practice*, 2nd edn, Brookfield, VT: Gower.

Peters, T. (1992) *Liberation Management*, New York: Knopf.

Pfeffer, J (1994) *Competitive Advantage through People*, Boston: Harvard University Press.

Poulsen, P.T. 1993 *Tænk det utænkelige. Revolutionen i Oticon* (Think the unthinkable. The revolution at Oticon), Copenhagen: Schultz.

Redding, J.C. and Catalanello, R.F. (1994) *Strategic Readiness*, San Francisco: Jossey-Bass.

Revans, R.W. (1982) *The origins and Growth of Action Learning*, Lund: Studentlitteratur.

Schein, E.H. (1992) *Organizational Culture and Leadership*, 2nd edn, San Francisco: Jossey-Bass.

Schlesinger, L.A. and Oshry, B. (1984) 'Quality of work life and the manager: muddle in the middle', *Organizational Dynamics* **13**: 5–19

Schuler, R.S. (1992) 'Strategic human resource management: linking the people with the strategic needs of the business', *Organizational Dynamics* **20**, Summer: 18–31.

— (1990) 'Repositioning the human resource function: transformation or demise?', *Academy of Management Executive* **4**(3): 49–60.

Sinding, T., Larsen, H.H., Gironda, L.A. and Sorensen, P.F. Jr. (1994) 'Back to the future: a pendulum in organization development',

Organization Development Journal **12**(2): 71–84.

Stähle, W. and Schirmer, F. (1992) 'Lower-level and middle level managers as the recipients and actors of human resource management', *International Studies of Management and Organization* **22**(1): 67–89.

Stewart, R.A. (1982) 'Model for understanding managerial jobs and behavior', *Academy of Management Review* **7**(1): 7–13.

Stuart, R. (1984) 'Using others to learn: some everyday practice', *Personnel Review* **13**(4): 13–18.

Torrington, D. (1989) 'Human resource management and the personnel function', in: J. Storey (ed.) *New Perspectives on Human Resource Management*, London: Routledge.

Watson, J.W. (1989) 'Human Resource Roles for the '90s', *Human Resource Planning*, March.

8

THE NEW FOREMEN ARE HERE![1]

Analysis of a myth

Philippe Trouvé

The present research is based on a series of studies performed by the author since 1987, particularly a questionnaire-based survey among the directors and the 154 foremen of seventeen French companies experiencing modernization processes in various fields of activity and a series of three biographical surveys (totalling eighty-two life stories) focusing on two subgroups of foremen (unskilled and promoted from workers' positions, and young graduates from short vocational upper studies such as the French BTS or DUT diplomas).[2]

During the last modernization phase, the weakening, if not the disappearance of line management, especially in its most traditional forms, was regularly announced. At the end of the 1980s, when faced with technological and organizational change, most industrial companies considered that they would have to get rid of foremen promoted from workers' positions, generally aged and poorly educated, to replace them with a new workforce, younger and more elaborately trained (especially at undergraduate level, that is to say, at BTS-DUT level).[3]

The first part of this chapter is dedicated to defining the object of this research. For the sake of clarity, only foremen in the industrial sector will be considered. Based on macrosocial data, the second part of the chapter reveals that both jobs and line managers did not evolve as expected. Even though the patterns of rejuvenation and lateral or direct access to supervisory staff positions cannot be denied, the 'traditional' model of internal promotion has persisted.

Two hypotheses can be invoked to explain this dual process. The first pinpoints the limits of a neo-classical approach to the labour market of middle management. It shows that the functioning of this market depends less on the laws of supply and demand than on mechanisms of social regulation. These mechanisms enable companies to use 'traditional' supervisory staff to maintain some kind of continuity and social and organizational stability at the very heart of their dynamics of change.

The second hypothesis focuses on the strategies of the new supervisory staff by analysing these actors' logic. The position of foreman is perceived as a transitory position, if not a regression when compared to the ambition of reaching management or exclusively technical positions. On the other hand, although the socialization process of these actors appears to be better adapted to new – and often idealized – productive paradigms than that of their seniors, they seem to find it difficult to use their technical know-how in traditional organizational set-ups. Paradoxically, while modernization of line management asks for codified and formally taught managerial competencies and techniques, it also relies on 'diffuse' know-how based on experience and internalization of the company culture. It is obvious that modern management does not eliminate these residual know-hows that traditional management masters.

The analysis of the recent evolution of categories of line management and of the actors' strategies that result from this evolution is a good reflection of the change processes under way in work systems. It reveals that, contrary to the most common mythical representations that managers have of present changes, the switch to a post-Taylor paradigm is far from complete and generalized, be it from the perspective of the line managers themselves or from that of organizations.

DEFINITION OF THE OBJECT OF STUDY

Although it is not our purpose to review the lists of line management jobs nor to define the positioning of supervisory staff in such classifications, our object of study needs to be defined. At least five points of view can be adopted. They do not entirely overlap and raise a series of questions that will only be evoked here.

Supervisory staff is first and foremost a statistical category which can be covered by the PCS 48 in the Professions and Socioprofessional Categories defined by the INSEE.[4] However, the relative position of supervisory staff in this classification has long remained ambiguous, and has been changed recently: classified under the category of 'Workers' until the census of the French population in 1982, it has since been moved to the category 'Intermediary professions'.

Supervisory staff also defines a sociological class. As such, it belongs to the 'middle class', which is known to play the role of an intermediary platform for upward or downward mobility.

Thirdly, it also defines a professional category, often designated as a 'buffer category' because of its intermediary characteristic. It comprises hierarchical levels or categories (first-level supervisory staff: team leaders, and second-level supervisory staff: foremen), various functions (for example: manufacturing, maintenance, warehousing and storing), or even heterogenous types of expertise (electrical-electronical, mechanics, building and public works).

Fourthly, it can be described as a statutory category with reference to the French classification system ('cadres') and to the collective union agreements. It is then labelled 'non-cadres' 'management category' – an expression which must appear mysterious outside France.

Finally, industrial supervisory staff could also be defined by its field of activity or its job content. From that point of view, a simple comparison between the very orthodox definition of the INSEE ('Foreman: agent having authority over other foremen or over workers') and that suggested by the Operational Index of Professions and Jobs (in French: ROME) of the Employment Agency (in French: ANPE) published at the end of 1993 would justify extensive comments in itself.

In the second case, in which only the generic term of 'supervisory staff' is retained, the hierarchy across categories is ignored (team leaders and foremen are no longer distinguished). Only the differentiation between three sectors, three functions or manufacturing modes, is taken into account: manufacturing/servicing, maintenance/process industries. According to this classification of the Operational Index of Professions and Jobs, 'supervisory staff':

- 'motivates and manages one or several teams according to directives'
- 'ensures technical assistance in the team'

- 'can be asked to use data processing equipment'.
                    (Agence Nationale pour l'Emploi, 1993)

This latter definition sums up all the ambiguities of the category under study, particularly its proximity to teamwork coupled with the role of hierarchical intermediary transmitting directives elaborated by other actors, managerial or motivational tasks and direct technical intervention.

FOREMAN: A THREATENED PROFESSION?

Since the end of the 1970s, productive systems and professional structures have experienced major changes in industrial countries. We will cover major transformations only to then consider the positioning of close management among these transformations.

A few recent transformations of socio-productive systems

Based on a classical analysis of major production factors, the identification of changes reveals:

1 A shift of industrial and capital profitability strategies thanks to new sources of competitivness such as differentiation, quality and innovation (of products as well as of processes) rather than volume or decreasing of manufacturing costs. This is referred to as 'global competitiveness' in the Ninth Economic Plan of the French Government.

2 A technological component linked to various types of automation based on an increasingly extensive and decentralized use of computer science, for both production and production management.

3 The discovery of the central role of the organization and its changes for competitiveness, especially thanks to the analyses of the 'Japanese model' of success that abounded in the 1980s These organizational changes can be linked to three processes described in management literature:
   - a systemic process of rationalization leading to increasing integration and interdependence of the principal stages of production, and in particular of manufacturing and product/process control
   - a tendency, often difficult to analyse, to lighten and flatten hierarchical structures

139

- and the replacement of a 'push system', (in which studies, conception and production determine the flows) with a 'pull system' propelled by the client.

  Despite these strong tendencies, organizational changes observed in companies remain mostly undetermined. Only vaguely do they resemble the idealized or purified models in management literature. More often than not, productive and complex combinations of 'computer-based neo-Taylorism',[5] post-Taylor and post-Ford re-professionalization' (Kern and Schumann, 1984) or 'qualified group work'[6] emerge within the same national system, in various fields of activity, or even in the same company.

4 Finally, as concerns the labour factor, an important evolution of types of employment and of the use made of the work-force, which could be described in terms of quantity as well as quality.

The evolution of employment structures and of the work-force

With regard to quantitative aspects, one may indicate:

- a strong drive towards the service industry and de-industrialization: the service industry accounts for 63.5 per cent of the work-force in France, including 30 per cent in the industrial field
- a regular and strong increase in the management population, especially in sales (up 42 per cent between 1982 and 1990), 'Intermediary professions' (except 'supervisory staff and foremen', whose number decreased by 1 per cent) and 'Employees'
- a decrease in the workers' population (especially the non-qualified) of 700,000 jobs between 1982 and 1990, especially in the automotive sector, mechanical construction, textile, and chemistry sectors.

In relation to qualitative aspects, several changes observed are unfavourable to traditional supervisory staff, especially

- a decline in direct work whereas indirect work has expanded
- an increasing interpenetration of direct and indirect work
- a global increase in the basic level of education, especially in

the working class, bachelor degrees and short professional university studies (such as the French DUT/BTS) being preferred to vocational training (such as the French CAP-BEP diplomas)

- a 'switch to a competency-based logic' (Zarifian, 1988) in work-force management and in the acknowledgement of qualifications. Qualifications are now measured against actually mobilized capacities in concrete work situations, rather than against the nature of the jobs and functions occupied
- among professional socialization factors, companies request ever-increasing psychological involvement from their staff. This would explain the considerable development and perfecting of new technologies in human resource management.

In such a context, foremen and the function they have occupied up until now appear to be threatened, for three reasons: first, they are surrounded by a better trained and more autonomous work-force and by technicians who control the most formalistic knowledge concerning production while also invading manufacturing. They then must confront, within their own category, competitors who have a better higher level of education coming from the technicians' category or from vocational diplomas such as the French DUT or BTS. Finally, they are confronted with a transformation of work cultures revealed by the recession and unrelenting decline of management by constraint.

For all these reasons, at the end of the 1980s, most company leaders predicted either that intermediary levels of supervision would disappear, according to the most radical, or be put aside when promoted from the working class, according to the most moderate, and in any case be replaced by a new generation of young graduates from two years advanced vocational training courses.

However, two series of statistics question these hasty conclusions: on the one hand, the data available in the census of the French population as well as the various national Surveys on Employment Structures produced by the INSEE; on the other hand, the Development Surveys of the Centre of Studies and Research on Qualifications (in French, CEREQ), which reveal the insertion and professional integration schemes of young graduates from industrial professional diplomas.

141

Table 8.1 Evolution of the supervisory staff and foremen category
from 1962 to 1990

Year	Total	Evolution %	% active population	% men	% women
1962	306 142		1.6	94.1	5.9
1968	363 216	18.6	1.8	92.9	7.1
1975	443 305	22.0	2.0	94.1	5.9
1982	545 536	23.0	2.5	93.4	6.6
1990	546 414	0.1	2.5	93.0	7.0

Source: INSEE, RP

Table 8.2 Distribution and evolution of the category
'supervisory staff–foremen'
(PCS 48) per field of activity

Field of activity	% 82	% 90	% evolution 1982–1990
Agriculture	1.6	1.3	−14.6
Food industry	3.6	4.0	11.9
Energy	7.7	8.1	7.3
Manufacturing industry	44.3	38.6	−9
Building and public works	16.3	16.1	−1.2
Services:			
Businesses	6.5	7.8	22.2
Trade services	14.8	17.1	16.6
Non-trade services	5.6	7.0	23.9
Total	100	100	0.2

Source: INSEE, RP 82 and 90

Line management: change and stability

As concerns the data, it testifies to:

- Stabilization of the number of supervisory staff, compared to a regular increase since 1962 – but not the predicted collapse (see Table 8.1). The trends differ from one sector to another. For example, if supervisory staff in the manufacturing industry has experienced a clear decline (–9 per cent) mostly due to the weakening of the workers' category in that same field, its size has grown in the food industry as well as in the fields of energy and services (see Table 8.2).
- Dynamics of hierarchical and functional restructuring – but inertia of the basic structure, for example, the first level (team

THE NEW FOREMEN ARE HERE!

Table 8.3 Evolution of supervisory staff (CS 48) between 1982 and
1990 by classifications

Classification	1982	%	1990	%	Evolution 1982–1990	%
2nd level*	113 816	20.9	146 173	26.8	32 357	28.4
1st level**	431 720	79.1	400 241	73.2	–31 479	–7.3
Total	545 536	100	546 414	100	878	0.2

Source: INSEE, Census

Notes:
* Second-level supervisory staff: shop floor, building site
** First-level supervisory staff: team

Table 8.4 Evolution of supervisory staff (CS 48) between 1982 and
1990 by functions

Functions	1982	%	1990	%	Evolution 1982–1990	%
100	398 764	73.1	344 325	63.0	–54 439	–13.7
200	91 208	16.7	120 181	22.0	28 973	31.8
300	34 112	6.3	42 224	7.7	8 112	23.8
400	21 452	3.9	39 684	7.3	18 232	85.0
Total	545 536	100	546 414	100	878	0.2

Source: INSEE, Census
Note: 100: manufacturing, building, undertaking
200: maintenance, new work
300: warehouse supervisor, storing
400: various supervisory tasks

leaders) seems to be the category most damaged by recent modernizations but it still employs 73 per cent of the whole supervisory staff category (Table 8.3). Similarly, jobs in direct manufacturing are fewer – but they still amount to 63 per cent of supervisory staff jobs (Table 8.4).

- A progression of the average educational level among the employment category 'supervisory staff, foremen' – but their relative weight in line management remains small (7 per cent of graduates of higher education).
- An increase in the supervisory population of less than 31 years of age (+ 3.2 per cent between 1982 and 1990) – but that population stands for 12 per cent of the supervisory staff 'only', while the 46 years of age and above make up 41.5 per cent of that same population.

143

Table 8.5 Jobs occupied by a graduate from short professional education: evolution between 1980 and 1988

Job categories	First job						Second job					
	Industrial DUT: year of graduation			Industrial BTS: year of graduation			Industrial DUT: year of graduation			Industrial BTS: year of graduation		
	1980%	1984%	1988%	1980%	1984%	1988%	1980%	1984%	1988%	1980%	1984%	1988%
Draughtsmen technicians*	41.2	50.4	55.1	37.8	43.5	56.1	52.6	53.9	58.6	49	49.6	62.5
Foremen *	3.3	2.1	3.3	1.8	3.0	1.8	5.5	3.4	4.3	4.3	4.5	3.6
Workers, other jobs	20.1	11.7	6.8	20.5	14.3	14.1	7.1	5.4	2.0	9	6.8	4.5

Source: CEREQ development surveys

Note: * excluding building and public works. The table reads as follows: 41.2 % of young 1980 graduates surveyed in 1984 have worked as draughtsmen or technicians in their first job; 3.3 % of the same population have initially worked as supervisory staff. On the other hand, 52.6 % of them have worked as draughtsmen or technicians in their most recent job, and 5.5 % as supervisory staff.

- As concerns the second point, that is, insertion schemes of young graduates from two-year advanced vocational training courses in intermediary professions, observations show that only a minority turn to, or are sent to, supervisory staff functions, whereas a majority end up in technical or planning department jobs, as shown by the Table 8.5.

Two interlinked questions come to mind. How can one explain both the competition between internal and external recruitment for staff supervisory positions, and the present permanence and resistance of internal promotion to supervisory positions? Why did the predictions of managers at the end of the 1980s which had foreseen a replacement of old-time supervisory staff not occur?

In order to answer these two questions, we use and successively distinguish two approaches: one relies on the functioning of the supervisory workplace; the other is more centred on the actors and their modes of professional socialization.

BROADENING THE NEO-CLASSICAL THEORY OF SEGMENTATION: FROM 'MARKET' TO 'SOCIAL REGULATION'

The economic theory of segmentation would reasonably explain the recent growth in competition between internal and external recruitment of a supervisory staff under change. Facing an increasingly uncertain and unstable environment, companies must increase their flexibility. They can achieve such flexibility by submitting their internal market (that is, supervisory staff and its constraints) more directly to the market pressure of the external work-force (that is, fresh graduates from the training system), considered to be better adapted a priori. This explanatory scheme would conform with managers' wishing to replace, for example, the old work-force with a new one.

However, our own research as well as macrosocial statistics demonstrate that this replacement scenario is far from being the most common today. Indeed, over the last years, companies have frequently chosen a more moderate type of management, mixing the two types of supervisory staff in various proportions.

This 'cohabitation' scenario must now be explained, as well as the persistence of access to supervisory staff through internal promotion. We believe that this requires the replacement of the

145

economic notion of a 'market' of supervisory positions with the more sociological notion of 'regulation'. It is well known that the classical theory that we will apply to supervisory staff is based on two main hypotheses:

1 By reducing the company to a black box and equating its functioning with the entrepreneur's rationality, the first hypothesis describes its behaviour as a search for optimization of its main production factors, especially the labour factor. From this point of view, when the company chooses a certain population to occupy supervisory positions, it simply makes an economic choice. Unless the theory is seriously amended, it appears very difficult to explain both the needs for the external market and the persistence of internal markets.

2 The labour market, like the market of goods, is believed to be ruled by the laws of supply and demand. Our hypothesis is that the market of supervisory positions does not function exclusively according to these laws. It reveals the existence of strong social and organizational regulations that reduce the scope of the power of the market. All things considered, as many have concluded before us, the labour market does not function in the same way as a market that is strictly submitted to the economic rationality of its actors.

What proves these two hypotheses false? How does the analysis of employment and the work-force illustrate the limits of the present neo-classical theory?

The invisible 'specific qualifications' linked to line management in the French context

1 The theory of segmentation would interpret traditional supervisory staff as an internal market, and the new supervisory population as a 'semi-qualified', if not 'professional' market (Marsden, 1989).[7] But even if the employer were to master total rationality, that is, the capacity for identifying the 'specific qualifications'[8] of each of the supervisory populations, the reasons to choose one or the other alternatively or simultaneously would be equal.

2 In France, a country that overestimates managerial capacity to the detriment of technical competency of supervisory staff, a

major part of the 'specific qualifications' that would lead companies to choose a certain profile of supervisory staff are social, and therefore difficult to assess. This phenomenon is all the more acute in France as the only qualification granted to line management is more socio-administrative (a 'label' without previous training) than technical and professional (as in the German context). In France, the absence of a national degree leading to the supervisory function banishes any clear identification of the required or acquired qualifications of line management.

3 It should be noted that the uncertainty linked to qualification applies just as much to traditional supervisory staff, for which the evaluation of the balance between costs and advantages is difficult to assess (high salaries at the end of careers – costs of informal, on-the-job training/stability and loyalty of this category), as to young supervisory staff from two years advanced training courses combining more moderate salaries and technical potential, but also an uncertain managerial capacity and a tendency to rotate jobs.

4 The ability of employers to make choices in terms of the recruitment of supervisors is limited by the technical and organizational changes that companies undergo. Indeed, the exercise of a supervisory function includes productivity factors other than direct physical productivity. It especially entails maintaining, if not producing, social cohesion as well as facilitating the commitment of operators beyond strict economic criteria. It follows that anticipating the behaviour of actors during a recruitment process cannot be achieved by strictly economic reasoning.

The market of supervisory jobs does not function like a 'market'

1 Logically, moving from a dualism of recruitment techniques as concerns supervisory staff (internal promotions versus external recruitment) to an authentic dualism of supervisory job markets would require the analysis not only of recruitment, but also of the changes in career management, compensation policies and training policies.

2 However, there is no evidence that internal and external markets of supervisory staff are partitioned today. For this

P. TROUVÉ

reason, it would be preferable to replace the notion of a 'dual' market by that of a 'mixed' market, which reflects the present cohabitation of the two types of supervisory staff in most companies. It must be pointed out that while companies increasingly resort to the external market, the market of supervisory positions tends to become more internalized. This phenomenon is linked first to the persistence of advancement through promotion, second to the employers' will to keep and stabilize young supervisory staff, and finally to the existence of two different markets, a promotional market within the internal market (traditional supervisory staff), and an internal market for horizontal mobility among young graduates with short professional diplomas who have spent two or three years in technical jobs.[9] Thus, the rigid distinction between the internal and the external markets no longer seems justifiable.

3 Technical and organizational changes are not as radical as is usually believed. They do not happen violently.[10] As a consequence, competition between the two components of supervisory staff (the young and the old) is not as acute as predicted. The search for new productive combinations forces companies into empirical and long-term adjustments which are not based on simple economic reasoning. Communication capacity as well as variables such as commitment, attachment or involvement, together with the search for some kind of social cohesion between various segments of supervision seem to play a central role.

As concerns psychological commitment, it is truly a 'joint regulation' (Reynaud, 1988, 1992) which mutually benefits both workers and employers. This point of view can be sustained within the framework of the economic theory. That is precisely what authors such as Akerlof (1984) or Williamson (1975) expressed when they dealt with employment relations in the long term, and based the power of the internal market on stability of relations between employers and workers (exchange of gift and counter-gift, loyalty, etc).

As concerns maintaining social cohesion, before or beyond division of work, one is led to reinterpret the company dynamics from the perspective of its community foundations.[11] Apart from strict 'efficiency rules', 'co-operation rules' (even implicit) exist

148

that hold the social body together (Reynaud, 1989: 76). These latter rules cover both the emergence of a new supervisory staff, closer to new organizational schemes, and the survival of an old supervision, guardian of stability, continuity and collective memory.

ACTORS' STRATEGIES AND RESTRUCTURING OF SUPERVISORY STAFF

The second set of arguments, that would reflect both the resistance of traditional supervisory staff and the weakness of the inflow of a younger and graduate population in supervisory positions, gives actors' strategies a central role. We base our analysis on a set of eighty-two true stories from both populations under study and elaborated within the scope of our personal research. This research aimed at, among other things, better understanding the modes of professional insertion and socialization of both populations, as well as the construction of their identity and of their professional ambitions.

The limits of the adaptation process of supervisory staff who face modernization are relatively well known. The 'crisis' of close management, almost as old as the category itself, has inspired many interpretations ('resistance (chronical, so to say) to change', 'role conflicts', or even 'class neurosis' or 'promotion neurosis') (Trouvé, 1993: 432, vol. 2). However, today, they are more linked to difficulties in revising identity, whether social or professional, than to an instrumental deficit.

The possible 'distinctive advantages' are equally well known: the rooting in the company's culture and know-how, the importance of which has paradoxically been acknowledged during the massive lay-offs of recent years; its psychological involvement, which can be interpreted as a form of dependency in a category that could be defined sociologically as an 'object' social group, but also as a guarantee of identification in the new context of 'membership management' (Aubert and de Gaulejac, 1991: 342). As one of our interviewees puts it: 'Working for our company is like working for ourselves.'

While organizational cultures changed quickly, promoted foremen seemed to experience a brutal decline in their distinctive advantages. Three main reasons justified, and still justify, the foreshadowing of the near disappearance of foremen: first, the erosion of self-taught cultures and of collective identities as a consequence of growth; second, the replacement of traditional empirical apprenticeship taught on the job by a professionalism based on technical, codified knowledge acquired through education; and finally, the necessary switch from management models based on stability and order to management practices based on change. But it has not been sufficiently ackowledged that even in the most modernized and productive structures, the mobilization of empirical know-how is still indispensable in most cases, whether in production, process or management technologies.

In other respects, the attitudes and expectations of new foremen played an important role in the slowing down of their progression in line management. Their individual – and some-times 'individualistic' – strategies actually strengthened the factors which contribute to the persistence of traditional foremen.

Based on our own data, two reasons could explain this last phenomenon:

1 On the one hand, the phenomenon seems to be linked to companies' observed failure to make organizational changes adapted to technological evolution. The gap between techno-logical modernization and organizational modernization is most definitely a 'French illness' (Linhart, 1991: 250). Con-sequently, the organizational context remaining unchanged, the supervisory positions offered cannot 'retain' young grad-uates with a professional education. 'If I feel confined and I have the opportunity of progressing elsewhere,' states a young graduate, 'I will go and progress elsewhere'.

2 On the other hand, the strategies of the actors themselves must be taken into account. Indeed, in most of the cases of young graduates interviewed, a position of direct supervision is per-ceived as essentially transitory. It is 'a springboard to move ahead', that is to say to move into a management position or a mostly technical job that would be more profitable in terms of career (conception, preparation, maintenance). Additionally, as concerns lifestyles, their position as individuals leads them to seek independence and to envisage their future outside the company ('I am not married to the company').[12]

From an interactive perspective combining the organizational logic and the actors' strategies, if their career path seems partially

coherent with the new (and often idealized) productive paradigms, the new 'generation' encounters a lack of professional
perspectives in more traditional organizations, since a supervisory staff position rarely leads to the status of manager. They
also encounter difficulties in mobilizing and using their technical
know-how, which is thought to be secondary in traditional
supervisory functions.

Moreover, even in organizations where technical and organizational modernization is well under way, uncertainty pertaining
to immediate management competencies of young graduates can
sometimes induce decision-makers to rely on 'vague' know-how
based on experience and the assimilation of a routine in which
traditional foremen can demonstrate their superiority. One could
illustrate that modern management does not eliminate these
'residual' know-hows mastered by the older generation of supervisors.

CONCLUSIONS

We sum up the three observations of our study as follows:

1 In the most recent phase of modernization, technical and
organizational transformations in companies suggested that
foremen and the most traditional populations of line management would be threatened in the long run.
2 However, although macrosocial data concerning industrial
supervisory positions during the 1980s do show that an
internal restructuring of supervisory jobs accompanied the
appearance of a younger and more educated work-force (especially from vocational education) and a simultaneous erosion
of the older faction promoted from workers' positions, these
phenomena did not take place on as large a scale or as quickly
as was predicted.
3 To illustrate the gap between managerial speeches and empirical data observed in the course of our own research, two
sets of hypotheses are suggested in summing up our third
observation:
• The first set shows that aspects of internal management
explain the functioning and the most recent trends in the
world of line management better than market mechanisms.
Only by stabilizing this world through a more or less

151

satisfactory joint regulation, did employers manage to combine the persistence of a supervisory staff promoted from workers' positions with the efforts to integrate new, educated foremen.

By maintaining when possible an unstable balance between two categories of supervisors and by avoiding the sacrifice of traditional supervisory staff, social regulation has preserved both community foundations, as well as the minimal level of social cohesion and continuity necessary in a company. It has also integrated supervisory functions with a salary relationship that makes global productivity dependent on the reinforcing of commitment, even loyalty, of the supervisory staff.

In organizations in which modernization is well under way, the new social and productivity conditions push companies to avoid sacrificing the socio-cultural balance to technological and organizational 'revolutions'. This explains the vitality of recruitment and internal promotion against all odds (Drexel and Fischer, 1990). We should not forget that the persistence of this internal recruitment channel does not do away with promotion from workers' positions, which enables either retaining the best performers among the workers (or the most 'deserving' ones) or offering them professional perspectives in the long term.

- The second set of hypotheses centres around socio-professional career paths of young foremen who graduated from short professional institutions. It shows that these young foremen are incited to neglect their line management tasks and to concentrate on promotional ambitions or hopes of gaining access to the status of manager or to strictly technical functions. Consequently, in their eyes, their position of foreman is transitory, if not regressive. They wish to leave it as soon as possible.

4 By the end of this demonstration, the replacement of traditional supervisory staff by 'new look' foremen appears to be more of a myth that confirms the gap between a modernist managerial discourse and the realities observed empirically in companies. This myth has grown from a double carelessness on the part of managers: first, as concerns the regulating capacity of a company and its community life and essence,

before or beyond the strict logic of efficiency. The pertinence of categories such as 'company culture', 'the social link', 'trusting relationships', 'loyalty' in an economy based on communication are being rediscovered. Second, as concerns the actors themselves (and especially the young graduates from vocational schools), develop professional strategies radically distinct from managerial expectations.

NOTES

1 'The new wine is here!' This promising expression, posted in most French cafés and restaurants, celebrates vintage wine every year.
2 In France, the two-year advanced vocational training courses are the Brevet de Technicien Supérieur, or BTS, and the Diplôme Universitaire de Technologie, or DUT.
3 We recall that in France, the Baccalauréat is granted as the achievement of high school studies.
4 INSEE: l'Institut National de la Statistique et des Etudes Economiques (the French National Institute of Statistics and Economic Studies).
5 This expression refers to types of technological modernization that cohabit with a persistence if not an accentuation of division of work.
6 Inspired from a Swedish scheme.
7 According to the author, 'the transferability of qualifications is the key characteristic of professional markets', whereas 'semi-qualified markets' rely on 'cross-company mobility, weak institutional regulation' (thus companies' difficulties in controlling this market, stabilizing and avoiding external rotation of its workforce) 'and a tendency towards externalization' (Marsden, 1989: 223, 222).
8 As Marsden (1989) does, we could define 'specific qualifications' as those for which – at least theoretically – competition is harsh among companies that are ready to pay an additional cost.
9 This internalization process could explain the weight of internal management on the behaviour of graduate foremen. Their sociological characteristics and their aspirations are closer to traditional supervision than to those of young foremen who graduated from short vocational upper studies.
10 These facts are established by our research on seventeen companies under a modernization process.
11 'The organization lives on and acts only thanks to the existence of an underlying community' (Reynaud, 1989: 79).
12 This capacity is linked to the transferability, at least theoretically, of their know-how.

REFERENCES

Agence Nationale pour l'Emploi (1993) *Répertoire Opérationnel des Métiers et des Emplois*, Paris: La Documentation Française. (See vol. I, p. 280; vol. II, p. 264; vol. III, p. 280; vol. IV, p.495.)

Akerlof, G.A. (1984) 'Gift exchange and efficiency wage theory: four views', *American Economic Review*, Proceedings, **74**: 79–83.

Aubert, N. and de Gaulejac, V. (1991), *Le coût de l'excellence*, Paris: Seuil.

Drexel, I. and Fischer, J. (1990) *L'entreprise et son rôle dans la qualification: création et développement de qualifications aux échelons intermédiaires en Allemagne et en France. Une comparaison.* Berlin: CEDEFOP (Centre Européen pour le Développement de la Formation Professionnelle), 52.

Kern, H. Schumann, M. (1984) *Das Ende der Arbeitsteilung?* Munich: Verlag C.H. (trad française).

Linhart, D. (1991) *Le torticolis de l'autruche. L'éternelle modernisation des entreprises françaises*, Paris: Seuil, coll 'Sociologie'.

Marsden, D., (1989) *Marchés du travail. Limites sociales des nouvelles théories*, Paris: Economica, 267.

Reynaud, J.D. (1988) 'Les régulations dans les organisations: régulation de contrôle et régulation autonome', *Revue Française de Sociologie*, **XXIX**: 5–18.

— (1989) *Les règles du jeu. L'action collective et la régulation sociale*, Paris: Armand Colin, 306.

— (1992), 'Quelques réflexions sur la régulation sociale', Paris, Ministère du travail, de l'emploi et de la Formation Professionnelle, *Convergence des modèles sociaux européens, 4ème séminaire sur l'Europe Sociale*, 8–9 October: 309–18.

Trouvé P. (1993) *L'évolution des agents de maîtrise face à la modernisation industrielle. Illustration à partir du cas français dans la période 1987–1993.* Clermont-Ferrand: CER-ESC CRA-CEREQ, Rapport au Ministère de la Recherche.

Williamson, O. (1975) *Markets and Hierarchies: Analysis and Anti-Trust Implications*, Glencoe: Free Press.

Zarifian, P. (1988) 'L'emergence du modèle de la compétence' in F. Stankiewicz (ed.) *Les stratégies d'entreprises face aux ressources humaines. L'après-taylorisme*, Paris: Economia, pp. 77–82.

9

MIDDLE MANAGEMENT AND QUALITY IMPROVEMENT
Evidence from five countries

Fotis Vouzas

INTRODUCTION

It is widely believed that the implementation of quality improvement programmes and more specifically the adaptation of a 'quality' philosophy is a driving force in achieving competitive advantage and survival in today's rapidly changing world business environment (Deming, 1986; Drucker, 1988; Peters and Waterman, 1982; Pfeffer, 1994). The emergence of Japan as a major world manufacturing leader, the decline of American products in the world markets and at home, and the increasing pressure for products and services that can fully satisfy customer needs brought quality to the front page of all the business and management periodicals and in the agendas of the chief executive officers. (Dale et al., 1993). During the 1980s an enormous amount of literature was developed in order to explain and analyse this new management philosophy. Several 'new' quality management prescriptions and schools of thought were developed, national organizations and awards were introduced, and numerous universities established courses on total quality issues.

Quality is no longer perceived as a product characteristic, but as a new 'management paradigm' which requires a cultural and behavioural change, and the involvement of all people within an organization (Crosby, 1979; Deming, 1986; Juran, 1964). One issue of great importance for the better understanding of this new management paradigm is the study of the relationship between the implementation of 'total quality approaches' and subsequently the examination of the 'quality level' an organization reaches and

155

the effect it has on the middle management roles. Most of the quality experts agree that this particular level of management is the key to the successful implementation of a total quality improvement effort and the keepers of a 'quality culture' (Collard, 1989; Dale et al., 1993; Ishikawa, 1985; Wilkinson et al., 1993).

It is argued that middle managers, being at the 'core' of the organizational structure, can play an important role and determine the success and the failure of total quality improvement efforts. On the other hand the implementation of quality programmes and the stage of quality which an organization actually achieves will have a major effect on the role and the nature of work of the middle managers. The main objectives of this chapter is to empirically test theory that links middle management roles with different levels or stages of total quality management. The main hypothesis is that the quality level or stage an organization achieves has a major effect on the way middle managers perform within an organization and subsequently determines their roles within that organization.

LITERATURE REVIEW

Definition of total quality management

It is generally accepted that organizations must view quality not only as a specialist and separate function responsible for inspecting and controlling the final products, but also as a management function and a vital part of organizational life span. During the 1980s and 1990s, an enormous amount of literature was developed on the subject of quality management. The majority of the writers were not academics but successful consultants, managers or engineers.

One of the major difficulties in studying total quality management (TQM) is the absence of a universal and generally accepted definition. According to Hart and Schlesinger (1991) there is a 'quality confusion' since TQM has existed as a management philosophy for only a few decades and in recent years many theorists and practitioners tried to equate the 'quality movement' with previous management movements or prescriptions, such as quality circles, QWL programmes, etc.

The writings of the well-known quality gurus such as Deming, Juran, Crosby, Peters and Ishikawa are considered to be the modern 'bibles' of today's TQM philosophy. Deming (1986) is well known for his fourteen points for management and his recent term 'Profound Knowledge', and Juran (1964; 1980) for his 'managerial breakthrough' approach for solving chronic problems and his trilogy concerning quality issues in organizations: quality planning, quality control and quality improvement. Crosby (1979) is associated with the 'zero defects' term. He developed a model for quality based on five absolutes for quality management. Peters (1982) regards quality as the main competitive advantage and defines quality as 'excellence'. Ishikawa (1985) on the other hand is the father of quality circles in Japan, and is well known for his seven quality tools and the distinction he makes between quality management in the Western world and Japan.

Looking at the TQM literature we can see that there are three different approaches and frameworks used to analyse and explain this new management paradigm. The first approach is based on the evolutionary view. Total quality is an approach to management that has evolved from a narrow focus on inspection, quality control, statistical process control, quality assurance to encompass a variety of technical and behavioural methods for improving organizational performance (Ciampa,1992; Dean and Bowen,1994).

The second approach takes a very critical view and suggests that TQM is conceptualized, not as a new paradigm, but as a comprehensive practice that captures signals from established models of organization and amplifies them by providing a methodology for use (Pfeffer, 1994; Spencer, 1994).

Finally there are the 'believers' of TQM. According to this approach TQM is a challenge to conventional management techniques and to the theories that underlie them. Therefore it cannot simply be grafted onto existing management structures and systems. Total quality management inevitably conflicts with established Western management practices. It's assumptions and theories are quite different from those underlying conventional practices, and therefore TQM will not succeed in a firm unless conventional practices are transformed (Ciampa, 1992; Grant et al., 1994).

Even though there are different approaches and consequently different definitions, there is a consensus regarding the basic principles, methods and practices of TQM. For the purpose of this study a model of TQM is produced in Figure 9.1. The model

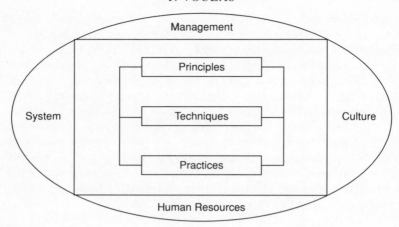

Figure 9.1 Total quality management: the new management philosophy

consists of the four fundamental blocks of quality management, human resources, system, culture and management, and in the centre of the model are the basic principles:

- focus on meeting customers needs
- everybody is responsible for quality – the concept of the 'internal and external customer'
- education and training are the cornerstones of every quality improvement effort
- measurement and feedback
- emphasis on continuous improvement
- top management commitment
- establishing closer relations with suppliers.

On the practices and techniques, which represent the 'hard' side of quality, are frequently elements such as:

- statistical tools and techniques
- implementation of quality systems
- production systems such as kanban, JIT, etc.
- quality function deployment
- process re-engineering
- failure-mode and effect analysis
- The seven new quality-control tools, etc.

All the above constitute 'total quality management', a most controversial management philosophy and approach for managers and academics today.

Levels or stages of total quality management

Several authors agree that organizations pass through several stages on their journey to quality improvement. According to Garvin (1984) quality has emerged at an evolutionary pace which could be put in a chronological and contextual order starting from inspection, passing to statistical quality control and quality assurance and, finally, reaching the the strategic quality management stage.

The UMIST approach (Dale et al., 1993), identifies six different levels/stages of quality management based on data drawn from British manufacturing organizations, which are 'characteristics and behaviours organizations display in relation to total quality management (uncommitted, drifters, tool-pushers, improvers, award-winners, and world class). Holmegaard (1990) describes principles for evaluating the effectiveness of quality systems suggesting three profiles/stages of quality systems. These quality system profiles characterize the development of an organization's efforts depicting stages through which a quality system may progress (profile 1: low degree of quality management; profile 2: some degree of quality management; and profile 3: high degree of quality management).

For the purpose of this study the author assumed that organizations implementing quality improvement efforts can be classified in four different stages which also characterize the level of quality improvement. The four stages are (see also Figure 9.2):

- **Stage One**: *Evidence of a specialist and separate function*. According to all 'quality gurus', this is the first step that all organizations go through in order to achieve a respectable level of quality.
- **Stage Two**: *Organization-wide special initiatives* such as quality circles, adopting the ideas and approach of one of the 'quality gurus', implementation of various continuous improvement teams and programmes, quality awareness sessions, etc.
- **Stage Three**: *Quality is integrated into organizational processes*. Implementation of quality assurance systems (such as the ISO 9000 series) and preoccupation with the 'hard' aspects of quality.

159

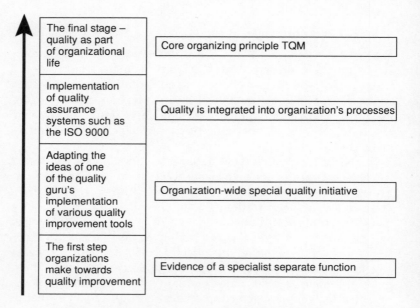

Figure 9.2 Levels or stages of quality management

- **Stage Four**: *Quality as the core organizing principle – TQM*. In this stage, all the above stages also are present, but are integrated and are part of a core organizing principle.

These stages must be considered as additive.

Quality improvement and middle management roles

It is necessary to divide the literature on middle management roles and quality improvement into two parts. The first part of the literature examines the relationship between middle management and quality circles which is more evidence/discovery based. The second part deals with middle management and TQM and it is more opinion/invented based.

The vast majority of studies on this subject suggest that middle managers and quality circles are incompatible. Dale and Barlow (1984) argue that the greatest resistance reported on quality circles is middle managers, and Dale and Hayward (1984) believe that lack of co-operation from middle management was the main reason for the unsuccessful implementation of quality circles in Britain. Ishikawa (1985) believes that middle managers must play an important role in the design and introduction of quality circles. Barra (1983), Bartlett (1983) and Cole (1980) all agree that middle managers feel alienated and have a feeling of loss of power closely related to the implementation of quality circles.

A pessimistic view is present in all studies on quality circles (QC) and middle managers. All writers suggest that the major blocking mechanism in the successful implementation of QC are the attitudes and behaviour of middle managers who feel insecure, lack knowledge and skills, and do not have the authority and support from top management (Brennan, 1991).

Hill (1991) found that quality circles disrupt middle managers' lives and create an organizational complexity that confuses existing structures and middle managers had no reason to make them work. Organizational complexity arises as a result of establishing quality circles as a parallel or dualistic structure which coexists with the normal organizational structure.

Very few empirical studies have been done examining the role of middle management in TQM organizations (Dopson et al., 1992; IPM, 1993; Wilkinson et al., 1993). The majority of the literature is opinion based and assumes a very broad role and more responsibility for middle managers. More specifically, middle managers in TQM organizations have the following 'roles':

- translating top management vision, strategy and mission into functional activities for the organization (Huge, 1990; Ishikawa, 1985)
- providing feedback to the top management concerning the status of the functional activities (Hand and Plowman, 1992; Huge, 1990)
- aligning top management's vision with the staff and workforce's individual needs (Deming, 1982)
- acting as coaches, facilitators, team leaders (Ciampa, 1992; Oakland, 1989)
- establishing competency models for the new behaviours

required in the successful implementation of total quality (Ciampa, 1992).

Ishikawa (1985) considers middle managers to be the key people in quality management and the key players in breaking the *status quo*. He calls this layer of management 'traffic policemen'. He believes that middle managers are at the crossroads, they have to obtain crucial information and acquire the ability to make judgements based on a broad perspective. For middle managers, according to Ishikawa, it is not necessary to stand always in the middle, meaning being always present. They in turn have to delegate authority to subordinates and use their abilities to the highest extent and grow in their jobs. Another role is that of teacher to his or her subordinates through on-the-job-training.

Research has shown that even though middle managers want to participate in the early stages of TQM, top management has no trust in them. They are reluctant to delegate responsibility and authority, and do not usually provide training courses for middle managers. One of the problems encountered in the implementation of TQM programmes is the lack of commitment from middle managers. Wilkinson et al. (1993) argues that lack of commitment from middle management has been the case in nine out of ten organizations they studied. The study also suggested that the effect of TQM on middle managers was substantial, made their jobs more demanding, emphasized team work, people management skills and technical knowledge. On the other hand they found that TQM does not improve their career prospects.

Another study by Marchington and Dale (1993) suggests that middle managers are concerned about a loss of authority or increased workload associated with TQM. Collard (1989) on the other hand found that in order for middle managers to be role models in a TQM environment they need to upgrade their communication and presentation skills, skills for working with groups and group leadership skills.

Hill (1991) in an attempt to study the differences and similarities between TQM and quality circles found that in organizations that evolved from QC to TQM, TQM had a positive effect on middle managers:

- helped them to manage more effectively
- increased their participation.

Middle managers were involved in the early stages of the TQM programme and had a key role to play. They acted as coaches, facilitators or as business co-ordinators and believed that total quality could advance their careers. He found that commitment from middle managers was very high and they were required to assist subordinates, encourage openness, consult before making decisions, work more on teams and trust and show respect to others.

THE RESEARCH METHODOLOGY

This study is part of the five-country survey (Chapter 4). A major part of the research project was the study of the relationship between quality and middle management roles.

The approach used here to analyse quality and middle managers was to determine the level or stage of quality improvement of the fifteen organizations in the five countries (see Table 9.1) and, based on this, to further study the effect it has on middle-level managers. For this part of the study extensive semi-structured interviews with quality managers, senior managers and middle managers in fifteen organizations covering two sectors (manufacturing and health sector), in five countries (the UK, France, Holland, Portugal and Greece) on quality issues were taken.

A closer view of the research methodology used in this study is thoroughly described in Chapter 1 of the book. In the first part of this section an analysis of the level or stage of quality management in the fifteen organizations is presented. The second part is a summary of qualitative observations and an analysis of the effect of the level or stage of quality management on middle management roles.

THE RESEARCH RESULTS

The stage/level of quality management in the fifteen organizations

Evidence of a specialist and separate function

Almost all organizations in the private manufacturing sector had a quality control or quality assurance department. However, in many cases the size and importance of the function was considerably reduced. In all Greek and Portuguese organizations, and in one French organization, quality departments were respectively large, well organized and autonomous, practising a wide range of quality activities.

In these organizations quality was perceived as a peripheral function and the role of the quality department was to monitor quality and maintain an acceptable level of 'quality products'. Co-operation among departments on quality issues was non-existent and conflicts between production and quality departments was a common phenomenon.

There was no evidence of a specialized and separate quality function approach in the public hospitals in the five countries. In the majority of the hospitals in the five countries a senior manager was assigned as a 'quality' manager. .The nursing functions in France and Portugal were trying to take responsibility and 'manage' quality issues. However, the nature of the work, the environment and the mentality of public hospital administrators are the main reasons why hospitals are not in this particular level of quality management.

Organization-wide special initiatives

Quality awareness sessions were very common in almost all fifteen organizations, but the implementation of organization-wide quality special initiatives such as quality circles, the adaptation of the theory of one of the quality 'guru's', and education and training programmes on quality issues was the primary tool for promoting quality within the organization in three manufacturing organizations (English, French, Dutch organizations). Several organizations in the manufacturing sector tried to implement quality circles but most of them failed. In the majority of the cases quality circles initiatives were either being abandoned or the participation levels were very low. There were several reasons for this, such as: lack of commitment from the top management, lack of resources put into the circles, no clear objectives and mission for the circles, no authority to middle management, fear from middle management.

In the public health sector several and various initiatives were reported such as the 'Projet d' Etablissement' in France, initiated by the Ministry of Health, the 'Project Personnel Management' in The Netherlands and some educational and training programmes concerning quality issues sponsored by the EU in

Table 9.1 The levels or stages of quality management in the five countries and the two sectors

Levels or stages of quality management	UK	France	Netherlands	Portugal	Greece
Evidence of a specialist and a separate function				M1	M1 M2
Organization-wide special quality initiatives	M2 H1	H1	H1 M2		
Quality is integrated into organizational processes		M1		M2	
Quality as a 'core' organizing principle TQM	M1	M2	M1		

Note: (M) = manufacturer, (H) = hospital

Portugal and, finally, several attempts towards new reforms in the UK National Health Service including 'quality' issues.

Organizations belonging to this particular stage or level of quality management were moved from the traditional and 'control'-oriented quality department approach to quality improvement, and were willing to adopt a wider perspective on quality improvement, but there is also a danger from the unknown as one Dutch managing director said. The majority of the organizations at this level believe that reaching a higher quality management level is one of their long-term goals.

The results are summarized in Table 9.1.

Quality is integrated into organizational processes

All organizations in the private sector had the ISO 9000 series certification. The certification was the 'main quality weapon' for the majority of the organizations. Most of the organization used the ISO 9000 certification as their 'quality strategy, mission'. The quality manual (necessary in order for organizations to obtain the certification) was the quality 'bible'. The production process and maintenance were certified in all organizations. The ISO 9000 series is considered by managers as inflexible, time-consuming and not a competitive weapon. The most common reasons for implementing ISO standards were, intense competition, demand by suppliers and customers, decision by top management, and as a way of organizing the quality efforts.

In the public health sector, there were no quality assurance systems in use, but in some hospitals there were written procedures, but these were not followed systematically. The hospital administration argued that writing procedures is time-consuming and they do not provide flexibility which is the main issue in hospitals. Procedures are in place in all hospitals but are informal in the organizations in our sample.

Core organizing principle: total quality management

Elements of a move towards a total quality management approach, meaning covering all the above stages/levels and the soft and hard aspects of quality (one British and one Dutch private organization), were found in only three organizations. The elements of TQM that were identified in these organizations, according to people interviewed, were:

- top management commitment to quality
- top management consider quality as a main management principle
- employee participation in quality; everybody in the organization was responsible for quality
- systematic and formal quality education and training
- implementation of a quality assurance system
- all functions participated in the quality efforts.

Total quality management, was not the term used in the two organizations. The organization refer to their approach to quality as 'quality improvement programme' and the Dutch as 'management of total quality (MTQ)'. The main reason was that the term 'TQM' was so extensively used in other organizations that these two organizations thought their approach was an 'internal organizational approach' and not another consultancy firm's package.

In the other organizations, TQM was an issue for consideration and a future target, for the remaining organizations (mainly French, Dutch and British) a way to manage in the future. In Greek and Portuguese organizations top management was sceptical about TQM and not fully aware of its principles, concepts, tools and methods, and philosophy.

In the public health sector, TQM is far from being a core organizing principle. In the French, British and Dutch hospitals there is a tendency towards a total quality management approach, but in Greek and Portuguese hospitals one cannot identify any encouraging practices or steps towards TQM the reason being that everything is coming through government regulations and the public hospitals are not yet ready for such an evolutionary approach.

Qualitative observations of the levels or stages of quality management and their effect on middle management roles

Since quality is one of the major driving force of organizations today, the study of the relationship between quality improvement level and middle management is of great importance if someone wants to fully understand how middle managers cope with quality and how quality affects middle managers.

In all the fifteen organizations, in the two sectors of the sample, the hypothesis of a reduction of middle management population due to design and implementation of quality programmes, initiatives or systems was not fully supported here. In the literature many authors argue that quality can reduce the numbers of middle managers, since quality improvement teams take over the middle managers role. A number of top-level managers argued (from the UK and The Netherlands) that ISO 9000 certification can reduce the number of middle managers but not the implementation of TQM, because in a TQM climate and philosophy middle managers are the key people, and it would be a disaster to reduce or remove them.

In the organizations moving towards a TQM stage middle managers felt closer to the organization and worked together with other colleagues and departments towards the common target – meeting customer requirements. In the organizations where quality was integrated into organizational process and the implementation of the ISO 9000 series was the main route to quality improvement, middle managers were responsible for writing down the procedures and establishing a climate for the implementation and support of the quality system (Portugal, France).

Middle management security seems not to be at stake in our sample because of the introduction of total quality programmes.

167

On the contrary, middle managers in the organizations which were in a TQM stage felt more secure than ever, having more responsibilities and authority than before. But in the organizations still at the first stage, middle managers felt insecure and the future implementation of a quality assurance system gives them a sense of uncertainty and fear. The perception of changes is according to the stage of quality implementation.

When the implementation of the ISO 9000 series was considered as a tool, the first step towards TQM, and part of a total quality approach and philosophy, middle managers felt more free to act, had greater authority, said that they were part of a team, and were sometimes team leaders. In the organizations with a strict and inflexible structure (Greek and Portuguese organizations) usually belonging to the first three stages, middle managers identified themselves as supervisors, with formalized lines of authority and a less autonomous role. Middle managers in these organizations were acting as guardians of well-kept territories. In one Dutch manufacturing organization, the assistant plant manager's main role was the supervision of the staff below even though several work groups were in operation in the plant and the company was practising several quality improvement initiatives.

In the majority of the organizations in both sectors, flexibility and creativity are in the hands of specialist departments or of top management. Organizations of the sample seems to choose a more stable and systematic approach to quality instead of creating the conditions for flexibility, innovation and creativity from middle management.

In organizations moving towards TQM, middle managers have more influence over quality issues and most of the time participate directly in the formation of the organizational strategy, either by submitting proposals, or by developing plans that fit into the organization's master plan (Dutch and British organizations). With the formation of quality improvement teams and with the pressure to get the best out of their people under a quality philosophy, the development of people-oriented skills was a major concern of middle managers. Top management in a TQM organization seems to expect more from these people. However, the majority of middle managers came to this level as a result of their technical competencies. This fact is working against middle managers, making them vulnerable and sometimes inefficient under the new circumstances. Total quality management organizations were trying to enhance middle manager's skills and competencies and develop these people so they could contribute more in the quality improvement efforts. The ISO 9000 series seems to demand still more technical skills and less managerial, even though in a few organizations (France and Portugal) middle managers were getting courses on management issues.

In several organizations of our sample middle managers were, according to top management, the key people (one Portuguese, English and Dutch organizations). With their unique position in the organization, middle managers are the people who mainly support and maintain all new quality initiatives or programmes the organization implements. For example, in the French hospital middle managers were the people responsible for the successful implementation of Projet d'Etablissement, and in the Dutch hospital middle managers were in the middle of the new organizational chart, that is, in charge of key issues such as budgets, resources and influencing people to adapt to the new situation.

In the case of organizations implementing organization-wide quality initiatives, middle managers were not, generally speaking, at the centre of the action. Top management was the main actor and middle managers were the people who traditionally translated the messages down to employees and were involved in routine paperwork. It was very clear in our study that, in organizations which were in the TQM stage or where quality was integrated into organizational processes quality, middle managers were acting more as 'business managers' and less as 'middlemen' from a hierarchical point of view.

Under quality management, organizations are encouraged to measure everything and cost reduction is one of the major issues. Bearing in mind that in a quality environment everybody is responsible for quality, middle managers have to prove that they can add value to the firm and find ways to reduce costs and increase efficiency. This philosophy is still in an early development stage in the organizations at the first three quality management levels in the manufacturing sector, and also apply to the majority of the public hospitals.

Middle managers in organizations operating under TQM are more frequently evaluated, targets are more precisely defined and, generally, they are more accountable than before. Under

F. VOUZAS

total quality management or under the third stage when ISO 9000 series certification is in place, middle managers have more work to do, new roles, and more pressure and stress is put on them.

CONCLUSIONS

The overall conclusion is that the level or stage of quality in which each organization is situated plays an important role in the analysis of the relationship between middle management and quality.

The introduction and implementation of a quality assurance system based on international standards set by ISO 9000 series was the main approach and 'road to quality' used by the majority of the organizations in the private sector. In the public health sector, quality, even though high on the top management agenda and always a very common language in the regulations or laws of the Ministry of Health, was not yet considered to be influential and worth investing time and effort on it. This means that only few hospitals introduced 'quality initiatives' or implemented quality programmes, or tried to write down the procedures assuring quality.

Total quality management, even though it was well known by all people in all organizations, was often considered as a 'new management fad'. Only two out of the fifteen organizations were moving towards a TQM philosophy, trying to adopt a new philosophy of management and change the existing culture, making quality a core organizing principle.

Increased commitment seemed to be very closely related to quality and in all stages of quality management, commitment is high in the majority of the organizations of the sample. Middle managers that survived the downsizing, delayering processes of the 1980s felt closer to the organization.

On the other hand, some of the hypotheses of the literature on middle manager's roles in quality movement, were not strongly supported in this study. Involvement of middle managers in the design, implementation and improvement of quality management issues seems to be only in a developing stage, even in the organizations that are moving towards a TQM stage.

There are national and sector differences in the answers to our survey but there are also some similarities among countries concerning the public health sector (Greece, Portugal, and to some extent France). In this sector, organizations are still very sceptical about TQM and several problems exist in order for the hospitals to design and implement a quality programme or system. Greece and Portugal are very slow in adapting and moving more closely to TQM. The existence of powerful and highly specialized quality control departments and also the focus and the preoccupation with the 'hard' aspects of quality management did not allow middle managers to abandon their traditional role. In France, the UK and The Netherlands the pace of change is to some extent faster than in the other countries. The adaptation of new roles and the development of the necessary skills from middle management seem to be prerequisites for a successful implementation of quality improvement programmes.

REFERENCES

Barra, R. (1983) *Putting Quality Circles to Work: A Practical Strategy for Boosting Productivity and Profits*, New York: McGraw-Hill.

Bartlett, B. (1983) 'Success and failure in quality circles: a study of 25 companies', Occasional Paper, Employment Relations Resource Centre, Cambridge.

Brennan, M. (1991) 'Mismanagement and quality circles: how middle managers influence direct participation', *Employee Relations* 13(5): 22–32.

Ciampa, D. (1992) *Total Quality: A User's Guide for Implementation*, Massachusetts: Addison-Wesley.

Cole, R.E. (1980) 'Will quality circles work in the US?' *Quality Progress*, July: 30–3.

Collard, R. (1989) *'Total Quality: Success through People'*, Wimbledon: IPM.

Crosby, P.B. (1979) *'Quality is Free: The Art of Making Quality Certain'*, New York: McGraw-Hill.

Dale, B.G. and Barlow, E. (1984) 'Facilitator viewpoints on specific aspects of quality circle programmes', *Personnel Review* 13(4): 22–9.

Dale, B.G. and Hayward, S.G. (1984) 'A study of quality circle failures', UMIST Working Paper 8403.

Dale, B.G., Lascelles, D.M. and Boarden, R.J. (1990) 'Levels of total quality management' in B.G. Dale and J.J. Plunkett (1990) (eds) *Managing Quality*, London: Philip Allan.

Dale, B.G. and Plunkett, J.J. (1990) (eds) *Managing Quality*, London: Philip Allan.

Dean, J.M. and Bowen, D.E. (1994) 'Management theory and total quality: improving research and practice through development', *Academy Of Management Review* 19(3): 392–418.

Deming, W.E. (1986) *Out of the Crisis*, Cambridge, MA: MIT, Centre of Advanced Engineering Study.

Dopson, S. and Stewart, R. (1993) 'Information technology, organizational restructuring and the future of middle management', *New Technology, Work and Employment*, **8**(1): 10–20.

Dopson, S., Stewart, R. and Risk, A. (1992) 'The changing role of the middle manager in the UK', *International Studies of Management and Organization* **22**(1): 40–53.

Drucker, P.P. (1992) 'The new society of organizations', *Harvard Business Review*, **70**(5) September: 95–104.

Garvin, D.A. (1984) 'What does "product quality" really mean?', *Sloan Management Review*, **26**(2): 25–42.

Grant, M.R., Shani, R. and Krishnan, R. (1994) 'TQM's challenge to management theory and practice', *Sloan Management Review*, Winter: 25–35.

Hand, M. and Plowman, B. (1992) *Quality Management Handbook*, London: Butterworth-Heinemann.

Hart, C. and Schlesinger, L. (1991) 'Total quality management and the human resource professional: applying the Baldrige framework to human resources', *Human Resource Management*, **30**(4): 433–54.

Hill, S. (1991) 'Why quality circles failed but total quality management might succeed', *British Journal of Industrial Relations*, **29**(4): 541–68.

Holmegaard, J. (1990) 'Industrial quality systems profiles', *EOQ Quality*, April: 5–7.

Huge, E.C. (1990) *Total Quality: an Executive's Guide for the 1990s*, Homewood, Illinois: Irwin Publications.

IPM (1993) *Quality: People Matters*, London: Institute of Personnel Management.

Ishikawa, K. (1985) *What is TQC: The Japanese Way*, Englewood Cliffs, NJ: Prentice Hall.

Juran, J.M. (1964) *Managerial Breakthrough*, New York: McGraw-Hill.

— (1980) *Quality Planning and Analysis*, New York: McGraw-Hill.

Marchington, M. and Dale, B. (1993) 'Who is really taking the lead on quality?', *Personnel Management*, April: 30–3.

Oakland, J.S. (1989) *Total Quality Management*, Oxford: Heinemann.

Peters, T. and Waterman, R.H (1982) *In Search of Excellence*, New York: Harper and Row.

Pfeffer, J. (1994) *Competitive Advantage Through People*, Boston: Harvard Business School Press.

Spencer, A.B. (1994) 'Models of organization and total quality management: a comparison and critical evaluation', *Academy of Management Review* **19**(3): 446–7.

Wilkinson, A., Allen, P. and Snape, E. (1991) 'TQM and the management of labour', *Employee Relations* **13**(1): 24–31.

Wilkinson, A., Redman, T. and Snape, E. (1993) *Quality and the Manager*, Corby: Institute of Management.

10

THE CHANGING PSYCHOLOGICAL CONTRACTS OF MIDDLE MANAGERS IN GREAT BRITAIN

Effects and reactions

Sue Dopson, Jean Neumann and Helen Newell

INTRODUCTION

The role of middle managers remains a controversial subject. The picture of middle management portrayed by many articles and by the business press is predominantly a gloomy one. Most writers describe the middle manager as a frustrated, disillusioned individual caught in the middle of a hierarchy, impotent and with no real hope of career progression. The work is dreary, the careers are frustrating and information technology, some writers argue, will make the role yet more routine, uninteresting and unimportant. Other writers claim that recent organizational change has enhanced the role of middle managers as they serve as strategic 'ambassadors' for downward and upward communication. We have been working on a variety of different projects exploring the changing nature of middle management work and, in turn, these claims. We draw upon these projects in offering some thoughts about how middle management jobs and careers are changing. Specifically in this chapter, we address the topic of how British middle managers are reacting to those organizational changes which affect their roles, responsibilities and careers. We analyse data using a conceptual framework which combines the 'psychological contract' with a 'double-bind situation'. From this analysis, we find evidence for three common

173

reactions from middle managers to their changing employment contracts: uncertainty, contrariness, and the double-bind. Finally, the chapter points to a number of conclusions and discusses areas in which the ideas in this chapter could be developed.

RESEARCH BASE

Our empirical material consists of relevant data selected from twelve case studies and four action research projects. Middle managers are defined as all those in managerial positions above first-line supervision and below top management, for example in large companies, below the divisional board. The case studies were undertaken during a project (1985–93), initiated and partially funded by the European Foundation for the Improvement of Living and Working Conditions, comparing six Western European countries according to the nature of changes affecting middle management jobs and careers, as well as middle managers' reactions to such changes. In the UK, eight wide-ranging studies were carried out in a diversity of organizations: two from the public sector, two from financial services, one computer company, and three manufacturing organizations. Four, more detailed, case studies were carried out in which additional material was gathered from a manufacturing company, a new public sector agency, and a distributor of automobile parts. An additional case study that took place in British Telecom in 1993, specifically looked at middle management careers and was funded jointly by Warwick University and Templeton College, Oxford.

The longitudinal action research projects were undertaken in the manufacturing sector, involving the researchers in frequent participant observation of comprehensive change efforts. The chemical plant, a paper company, an engineering services firm, and an interior buildings supply manufacturer included two multinationals, one group of companies, and a small enterprise. Researchers were paid by the organizational clients to provide assistance with the organizational changes as well as to carry out research tasks.

Accumulated data available for this chapter, therefore, included over 500 semi-structured interviews and case study material from all seventeen sites as well as longitudinal field notes from four sites. These notes provided triangulation for the semi-structured, self-report interviews by introducing extensive observational and archival data. Researchers collected data for twenty-four days over a one-year period in the shortest project and for a maximum of 200 days over a five-year period in the longest project. Data analysis took the form of iterations of content analysis in order to answer a series of questions: what types of organizational changes are being undertaken; how are these changes affecting middle managers' contracts and how are middle managers reacting to these changes?

For examining types of organizational changes, we reviewed conclusions from previous analyses of the case studies and compared the four action research projects with them. Data from all sixteen sites were included in determining changes to middle managers' contracts. At that point, we selected data from four of the case studies and three of the action research projects to study middle managers' reactions and responses from their companies. Data from these seven sites contained the most lengthy and articulate descriptions of emotional responses from middle managers. The section of this chapter that discusses careers draws on one site, British Telecom (BT).

CHANGES TO MIDDLE MANAGERS' CONTRACTS

The executives and senior managers interviewed in our sites acknowledged that middle managers, in particular, have been affected by the degree and complexity of organizational changes. In particular, intensification of international competition, changes in the demographics and of relationships within families, and changing attitudes to authority and employee loyalty were cited. In response to these changes, organizations have often restructured, decentralized, expanded computerization and changed their managerial style from being autocratic to being participative or 'empowering'. In order to implement changes and respond to such pressures senior managers require middle managers to operate according to a new contract.

In an attempt to explore in more depth the degree of change in middle managers' jobs, we selected the concept of the 'psychological contract'. Its usefulness was as an initial tool for clarifying the multi-dimensional changes to the role of the middle manager more precisely without having to go into the degree of detail necessary with job design concepts. Also, by definition, the idea of a contract provides a link concept between the individual and the organization (see Kotter, 1982; Louis, 1980; Nicholson and Johns, 1985; Rousseau, 1990; Thierry, 1984). Of special relevance to us in understanding middle managers' reactions were applications of psychological contract to research on socialization (Wanous, 1980) and job satisfaction (Gowler, 1978; Mumford, 1978). We conceptualize organizational change as, in part, an attempt by senior managers to resocialize middle managers into new ways of behaving.

Originated by Argyris (1964), the concept of psychological contract has been developed most fully by Schein who offers the following definition: 'The set of unwritten expectations between an individual employee and the organization' (Schein, 1980: 22). He notes that the psychological contract is the essence of the linkage between individual and organization: employment entails an implicit exchange of beliefs and expectations about what constitutes legitimate actions by either party.

Rousseau has argued that as perceived obligations, psychological contracts differ from the more general concept of expectations because contracts are promissory and reciprocal. Promises of future behaviour on the part of the employer are contingent on some reciprocal action by the employee (Rousseau, 1990: 390). She gives an example:

> Company policies stipulating that employees who success-
> fully complete a ninety-day or six-month trial period are
> to be designated 'permanent employees', promise job
> security in exchange for satisfactory performance as a
> newcomer. In the case of contractual expectations, the
> promise of reciprocity in exchange for some action or effort
> is the basis of the contract
>
> (ibid.: 390).

Promises, therefore, need not be made explicitly. Rather, expectations formed during interactions regarding future patterns of reciprocity constitute a psychological contract. In other words, a psychological contract exists when individual employees believe they are obligated to perform in a certain way and that the employer has certain obligations towards them (ibid.: 390).

To get at the multi-dimensional changes to the middle managers' psychological contract that our interviewees had talked to us about, we drew on the works of both Mumford and Schein. In her research on job satisfaction, Mumford built on Talcott Parson's analysis of pattern variables to delineate five areas which comprise an employee contract: knowledge, psychological, efficiency, task and ethics (Mumford, 1978: 20–1). Mumford argues that if an employee's needs in these five contractual areas are met, job satisfaction will be high. Furthermore, if an employing organization's needs in these five areas are also met, then that firm should be satisfied with the performance and attitudes of its employees. This she describes as 'a mutually beneficial work environment for both sets of interested parties' (ibid.: 22–3).

We found this conceptualization of contract very useful but a bit too rational and objective for the degree of subjective, emotional reactions we had obtained from our interviewees. Mumford lists psychological contract as one of her five elements. We felt that all aspects of an actual employment contract could be conceived of as having psychological implications. This was supported by Schein (1980) who vividly describes and explains the processes by which organizations systematically socialize graduates of management schools into altering their expectations to be more in line with their employers. The subtle and frequently covert sanctions applied by more experienced managers on the new recruit struck us as more similar to the processes that take place during comprehensive organizational change. Schein also contributes the distinction between those aspects of organizations which are primarily collective, therefore common throughout all middle managers, and those aspects which are unique to the individual manager.

We combined Mumford's and Schein's work into a model of aspects of the psychological contract which might be changing for middle managers. We used this model to analyse statements made by middle managers and their employers in which they describe their expectations before and after significant organizational changes. Figure 10.1 contrasts their perceptions of the old and new contracts. We go on to describe the model adapted from both Mumford and Schein's work and summarize the data under each of the five elements.

Knowledge contract

The knowledge contract comprises the organizational aspects of recruitment, training and development, combined with the

177

OLD PSYCHOLOGICAL CONTRACT	EMERGING PSYCHOLOGICAL CONTRACT
KNOWLEDGE	
Demonstrate specialized expertise or gain professional qualifications.	Gain capability in general management areas like finance, information technology, etc.
Establish and maintain systems and routines in area of specialism.	Assist operational personnel to monitor and maintain systems in area of specialism.
Focus primarily inside one's employing organizations.	Focus simultaneously on outside relationships and inside the organization.
MOTIVATION	
Plan career in terms of upward promotions.	Avoid rewards which add layers of hierarchy.
Equate responsibility with span of control.	Equate responsibility with meeting performance targets like quality.
Be seen to balance home-life and work-life.	Be seen to work long hours on behalf of employer.
GOALS AND MEANS	
Maintain 'status quo'.	Look continuously for ways to innovate and improve.
Follow written procedures or custom and practice.	Take risks and experiment with any means necessary.
Work towards broad, general goals within professional specialism.	Meet budget vs performance targets regardless of one's specialism.
ROLE BEHAVIOURS	
Exercise authority in the benign dicatorial style.	Exercise authority in a participative, empowering style.
Focus primarly on the needs of one's own area of responsibility.	Co-operate with other departments in achieving organization-wide goals.
Use one's own wit and initiative to judge performance.	Use measures through information technology to judge quality and quantity of output.
ETHICS	
Differentiate personal values from organizational values.	Join personal values to organizational values.
Maintain privacy outside the organization.	Be seen to be publicly committed to organizational mission and ethos.
Live the organization ethics but don't talk about it.	Publish ethics statements.

Figure 10.1 Five elements of middle manager's psychological contracts

individual's degree of desire to use their knowledge and skills. Prior to the types of changes described above, a specialized expertise or area of professional knowledge was expected by employers, with the requisite qualifications. It was then the middle manager's job to ensure that appropriate systems and predictable routines were established to plan, implement, and evaluate the application of that knowledge to those aspects of the organization involved with the specialism.

However, the changing knowledge contract is towards more generalized management. Hence, middle managers experience increasing pressure to embark on management development programmes, often leading to a general management qualification. They are being obliged to develop qualities not linked to specialisms, specifically: the abilities to deal with continuous change and uncertainty, to forge and manage complex relationships both inside and outside the organization, to use initiative in meeting increasingly difficult and broad-based goals, and to use information technologies. Less and less do middle managers expect, and are expected, to follow detailed guidelines to the letter and to be rewarded for knowledge unique to their area, products, or people.

Motivation contract

Implicit in the employment relationship, and inseparable from it, lies the expectation that both employee and employer are induced to act in ways which establish a relationship between them for the related purposes of effort and reward. The motivation contract strikes this effort–reward bargain and includes the individual's unique reasons for motivation and stage of career and life cycle as well as the organization's need for a functional degree of employee morale and job satisfaction. Prior to the 1980s, the prospect of regular moves up a clearly defined, progressively narrowing career ladder operated as an important source of motivation for middle managers. Technical knowledge was rewarded with supervisory responsibility, and it was possible in most of our sixteen sites to succeed as a middle manager and relate predictably with others in one's personal life.

The context of drastic removals of hierarchical layers within most organizations shapes an emerging new motivation contract. Middle managers are now required to expect redundancy and/

or multiple opportunities for progression which are not neces-sarily hierarchical. For example, lateral promotion supported by separate technical and supervisory ladders are becoming increasingly common, vacancies are as likely to be filled by grad-uates or managers from other organizations as internally and regular disruption to one's personal life has become a norm. Increasingly, middle managers must let go of expectations of being developed, and of being valued for their accumulated developments, over a couple decades of their career. In a changing organization, people with histories firmly rooted in an earlier stage of the organization can be experienced as a liability by executives and senior managers.

Goals and means contract

A main aspect of socialization for a middle manager has to do with adhering to 'the way things are done here', usually in refer-ence to the norms about how one relates to authority figures and to issues of territory and time. The goals and means contract includes expectations about the basic goals of the organization and the preferred means by which those goals should be monitored and attained, including the individual's concerns with work controls and support services. The old contract empha-sized maintaining the *status quo* by closely following written procedures or custom and practice and by seeking permission for any decisions or actions out of the ordinary. Goals were set broadly and varied primarily within a recognizable set of constraints. Leadership on achieving targets was a role delegated upwards to executives or senior managers.

The new goals and means contract alters both the nature of goals and the means to achieve them. Innovation and improve-ment are the means of attaining goals which change dramati-cally as often as once a quarter. Performance and measurement systems are being introduced which allow executives to hold subunits and individual middle managers accountable for meeting targets. Often those targets require co-operation across functions and with sections of the organization over which one has no structural influence. The new minimum is 'continuous improvement' of targets; the middle manager must identify continuously areas of improvement and must be seen to be taking actions to implement those improvements. Maintaining a *status quo* is sometimes considered to be the equivalent of resisting change. Certainly, the complaints about middle managers' resistance points to the importance of these roles in implementing comprehensive changes. Not only are middle managers frequently assigned responsibility for project management, but they still constitute a crucial link in the chain of communication and command for implementation. Furthermore, the interconnections between multiple simultaneous initiatives within comprehensive changes (Neumann, 1989) often involves a middle manager in more than one change project. Clearly, given the increasing width of their span of control a negative middle manager can be a major barrier.

Role behaviour contract

Inherent in the exchange which takes place between an individual middle manager and the employing organization are accumulated expectations about how managers behave throughout society, and in the employing organization especially, as figures of responsible authority. The role behaviour contract includes basic responsibilities being granted to someone in a managerial role as well as standards of behavioural conduct being expected in return. Probably the most confusing changes to the middle management contract concern role behaviours. Supervising in an autocratic style and respecting the chain of command used to be mandatory for a managerial post. One managed a function, department or area according to one's own wits and judgement, limiting initiative to precise instructions from above. Disregarding the goals and needs of peers was essential to survival in competing for scarce resources. In short, administration of an area in a manner considered suitably managerial were the main expectations of the job.

However, the emerging role behaviour contract turns many of the old expectations upside down. Middle managers are expected to involve their employees, to inspire them to self-management and to coach them into taking on more responsibilities and initiative. Authoritarian behaviour is frowned upon. As long as the needs of customers are met, managers are now required to co-operate across departmental and subunit boundaries rather than compete. Taking initiative and not asking permission is the sign of someone with 'good management material'. Indeed, information technology makes it possible to delegate administration down the hierarchy, leaving – at least theoretically – the middle manager free to demonstrate enthusiasm and commitment to the values and mission of the organization, as expressed by executives and senior managers.

Ethics contract

A less commonly recognized aspect of the employment relationship concerns moral principles or rules of conduct which are more broad than the actual role in which the person is employed. The ethics contract pertains to the maintenance of the public identity and integrity of the organization. Including those values and work considered pivotal by the employer, ethics also refers to the beliefs of individual employees and the qualities which they value. The old contract provided for a significant degree of separation between personal and work values except on obvious personal descriptions, like one's marital status and consumption of alcohol. An individual would expect to keep to oneself those personal values out of harmony with corporate policy. It was felt that individuals could take pride in an efficient and productive employing organization. Privacy was not considered inconsistent with organizational goals.

The emerging ethics contract demands a greater degree of more visible commitment from middle managers at a time when society recognizes, and supports, the individual's ability to hold complex and contradictory values. Holding one's 'real self' outside of the organization used to be expected; now it is considered undesirable to the survival and success of the company. Looking beyond the confines of the area which they manage, middle managers now must be seen to be committed to the future of their employing organization and to its mission and goals. A cynical bureaucratic may have been perceived as functional by executives two decades ago, but not any more.

MIDDLE MANAGEMENT CAREERS

As a result of the changing psychological contract, a number of important questions arise with respect to middle management careers. For example, what role does the provision of an attractive replacement for the traditional career model play in the maintenance or renewal of commitment? In a climate of continuing job losses, is fear now the basis for an apparent renewal of commitment to the organization evidenced particularly in the reported greater intensification of work and longer hours of work for middle managers? If so, does this have a differential impact on the careers of male and female managers? Newell and Dopson (1994) are beginning to explore these questions in a project on middle management careers.

In the first case study of the project interviewees felt there was a lot of talk about career paths within the organization, some even felt that senior management thought that the formal systems were working. Only a few were optimistic that they would make some progress career-wise within the next few years. Most expected to 'muddle through'. The general feeling was that middle managers are staying with BT because they earn a relatively good salary and, relative to other organizations, they have a measure of security, although this was thought to be fragile. Of interest for this chapter are the strategies that the sample of middle managers in BT said they had pursued in response to their changing psychological contract. These strategies had little, if anything, to do with organizational systems and reveal a complete breakdown in the formal career planning systems. Such a range of strategies merits further research and is not a phenomenon discussed in any depth in the literature on careers.

Networking

Many interviewees commented on the fact that it was not the formal systems that were important, but rather one's contacts within the organization. For example: 'How you get on in BT is by who you know rather than any structured plan'; 'It was a case of picking up on what I have got to do, and also making contacts and getting to know the people and instilling in them faith in me'; 'You get on by being a friend of a friend. Senior managers are now surrounded by their chums, which is a dangerous situation'.

The influence of a particular senior manager could have a very great effect on career prospects in terms of who was recommended for vacant jobs. The most important person in terms of networking was often the middle manager's own line manager:

'The single most important thing in getting moved around, was eventually having a manager who took an interest in you.'

Visibility and networking went hand in hand, in that it was the key to being 'seen' doing your job and doing it well: 'It is all about visibility. I am trying to get organized so that I can have three days in the office shifting work. I want two days out of the office, one to make myself visible to the people who work for me, and one to make myself visible to the people I work for.'

Furthermore, it made a difference whether or not you were in the regions or in London, the headquarters of the organization. In terms of visibility the headquarters seemed to be the place to be. Outside London the chances of being able to network or being seen by the right people were very small and the chances of promotion thus limited: 'I knew I had to get to London. In London they tend to promote people more.' In fact, none of the interviewees in London were willing to consider a move to the regions and most of the interviewees in the regions would have welcomed the opportunity to be in London.

Luck and personal drive

Rather than there being a 'collaborative dialogue' it was often commented on that luck and/or personal drive were the important factors. Being in the right place at the right time was seen to be the key. 'It is wrong to talk about strategies, it is pure luck what happens to you in BT.' 'It's pure drive, it's personal ambition, it's being in the right place at the right time.' 'I was the driver in all my moves within BT except one, and that was luck.'

Exit

There were three comments that BT saw careers 'only occurring within BT' and refused to consider that some managers may go on to careers outside the organization. However, for a few managers the only option they felt they had, either to improve their job position or to feel more content as individuals, was to leave BT. One interviewee summed up the extent to which a mismatch between his and BT's expectations (a breach of the psychological contract) had affected him and his work and the difficulties surrounding the decision that he had made:

> In order to manage my career, I really had to leave, I want to take control of my work experience ... I went home drained and unhappy at BT because I gave people what they wanted ... I worry how I will be seen by other employers, but I hope it brings out some of the qualities in me that haven't really been required to be exposed ... I want to test my ability to handle change and uncertainty.

However, very few of the sample had been tempted to look outside BT for jobs, partly this may be explained by the managerial labour market. However, for the majority, BT was considered to be a good employer and staffed by good people: 'I think the company for me is the people you have worked with, that's where your loyalty springs from.'

The evidence from the case study that looked at middle management and careers suggests that we should be wary of drawing simple distinctions between optimistic and pessimistic scenarios for middle managers' careers. In this case, while the organization prescribed to an optimistic view of middle management careers and had developed various formal policies concerning them, such as personal development plans and individual career planning, the reality as perceived by middle managers themselves was of a much more pessimistic situation. The language of HRM being used by senior managers in the organization masks the reality of the situation for middle managers although the formal career management processes exist in a sophisticated form on paper, in practice they have ceased to operate in a situation where reductions in wastage and turnover have simultaneously reduced opportunities for internal job moves and led to a high degree of uncertainty over careers. Meanwhile, the ensuing vacuum has been filled by a variety of responses from individual middle managers who rely heavily upon what can be termed 'informal' systems of career planning.

MIDDLE MANAGERS' REACTIONS

How do middle managers react, then, to the numerous changes in their psychological contracts in terms of expected knowledge, motivation, goals and means, role behaviour, and ethics? In discussing this phenomenon, we noted the frequency with which they spoke of dilemmas facing them as a result of changes.

Dilemmas of a 'damned if I do, damned if I don't' variety suggested the potential usefulness of Gregory Bateson's (1972) concept of the double-bind situation.

A double-bind situation is one in which, no matter what a person does, he or she cannot win. This terminology, and a subsequently extensive programme of research, was initiated by Bateson to explain some individual's seriously negative reactions to contradictory communications. Bateson postulated that certain conditions were necessary to differentiate between those people who were aware of the contradiction, demonstrating an ability to differentiate conflicting logics in a message, and those people for whom such a contradiction led to dysfunctional, possibly self-destructive, behaviour.

We hoped to develop a better understanding of the strong emotions generated by 'damned if I do, damned if I don't' situations. Even so, it seemed unlikely that all managers would react similarly to the same types of changes. Not all managers would experience all changes from the old contract to the new contract as that significant, nor as a double-binding experience. Taking guidance from Bateson's theory, we hypothesized that those middle managers who had a longer history in an organization and who were at a later stage in their career would be most likely to experience changes as double-binding. This is based on the assumption that an older, more established employee would consider leaving the organization as an inconvenience, at minimum, and as an impossibility, in many cases. Further, he or she would have internalized organizational sanctions against open discussion with superiors.

We anticipated that two other types of negative reactions from middle managers were theoretically possible in addition to the double-bind. Some employees would experience contradictory changes as simply contradictory, without the corresponding feelings of not being able to discuss the situation openly or of not being able to exit the organization. Further, some employees would have an even milder reaction, but still one that would be experienced by senior managers, and themselves, as negative. We thought a sense of uncertainty in the face of contradictory messages was likely.

Thus, we speculated that an analysis of our data would result in a three-point continuum of negative responses from middle managers. The middle manager with the least seriously negative

	UNCERTAINTY	CONTRARINESS	DOUBLE-BIND
Stage of career	Early to mid-career	Mid-career	Middle to late career
Function	Staff	Line or Staff	Line
Problematic changes	Daily operative procedures Career Motivation	Increased responsibility and accountability Decreased resources and power	Loss of status and power New technology Authority relationships
Number of contract elements	2 to 3 elements changed	3 elements changed	2 to 4 elements changed
Coping strategies	Emphasize knowledge and expertise	Active or resistance challenge senior management	Passivity Give impression of conformity with angry outbursts

Figure 10.2 Three types of negative reaction from middle managers

response to contradictory messages from senior management would feel uncertain. The next most serious reaction would be contrariness. And, the most serious of all would be that middle manager who experienced him or herself to be in a double-binding situation.

We also anticipated that the comprehensiveness of the organizational change would be a factor in influencing the degree of negativity felt by a middle manager. We reasoned that part of what defines a complex organizational change is the fact that many organizational variables are subjected to change, therefore, the more complex the change, the more aspects of the middle managers' contracts would be changing. In short, we believed that middle managers would react more negatively in situations where more aspects of their psychological contract were changed. Figure 10.2 offers a matrix of the conceptual framework and a summary of the data analysed.

Uncertain

The middle manager with the least negative reaction feels uncertain. He or she feels confused about the change, lacking sufficient knowledge and understanding to be able to take a clear stand one way or the other. He or she may express annoyance at senior managers for their lack of clarity in communication and for their lack of sensitivity about what their middle managers need in order to co-operate with a change. The following quotation from a BT middle manager illustrates an uncertain reaction: 'Depending on where you are in the organization, you get a different message. The biggest constraint is trying to move forward in an environment where the overall message about where we should be going is unclear.'

The majority of middle managers in our data who reacted uncertainly to organizational changes were in early to middle career and worked mostly in a staff function. The changes they experienced as problematic were those which affected the way in which work was carried out on a daily basis and those which affected their motivation. Career prospects were explicitly mentioned. Between two to three elements of their contracts were affected by the changes. Emphasizing their knowledge and expertise and working harder were common coping strategies.

Contrary

The middle manager with a middle range negative reaction feels contrary. He or she feels angry about the change, noticing the self-contradictory or essentially absurd aspects of the change. He or she may express opposition to senior managers for their unreasonable decisions and for their illogical ability to see the mutually opposing situations in which they have placed their middle managers. An example of a contrary reaction, again from a BT middle manager, is: 'The company says that the key task for middle managers is to develop his or her people, yet, when we try to do this, the issues of managing our budget is raised. So the signals are there and these other targets frankly get in the way.'

The majority of the middle managers in our data who experienced the changes as contradictory were in middle career and worked in both line and staff functions. The changes which they experienced as problematic primarily had to do with increased responsibilities and accountabilities with a corresponding decrease in resources and power. While career was mentioned, it was not predominant as with the uncertain managers. Three was the most frequent number of changes to their psychological contract. A few contrary managers report an acceptance of change and trying to manage the situation regardless of their emotional reaction. The majority, however, engage in some form of active resistance or challenge to the senior managers.

Double-bind

The middle manager with the strongest negative reaction feels caught in a double-bind. He or she feels constricted about the change, being forced to choose between two equally undesirable alternatives. For example: 'They say that I have more responsibility and I am more accountable. But accountability is measuring what you're doing and then doing it and the changes have brought none of the expected freedoms that go with additional responsibility' (BT manager).

Or, he or she may express passive resistance towards senior managers for their role in creating the changes in the first place and for retaining the power to sanction middle managers as this quote illustrates: 'You build a paper house, you tell senior managers that you have built it to satisfy them, then you start laying the bricks so it does not fall down.'

The majority of middle managers in our data who reacted severely to the organizational changes were in middle to late career and worked mostly in line functions. The changes they experienced as problematic emphasized loss of status or loss of power to carry out their work. Pressures to learn new technology and new approaches for exercising authority led to feelings of insecurity and resentment. Between two and four aspects of their contracts were implicated in the changes. The preferred coping strategy appears to be passivity with occasional bursts of direct anger at senior managers. This group of managers give the impression of conformity, while hoping for a change brought either by retirement, exit from the organization or the hope that change is a passing fad.

Our judgement as researchers as to the degree of emotional negativity did not always bear out in terms of those individuals' coping strategies. There are, as discussed above, trends in reported coping strategies: uncertain middle managers emphasize the importance of expertise and work harder; contrary middle managers resist actively; double-binded middle managers resist passively. Even so, not all managers cope similarly. The strongest similarity was in the double-bind category.

We think this congruence among middle managers who experience the organizational changes as a double-bind situation can be explained primarily due to the fact that they are in middle to late career. They do indeed have characteristics in common with Batesons' analysis: inability to leave the contradictory situation and inability to discuss the contradiction. Emotional and financial investments in a particular locale and retirement scheme increases the risk of leaving the organization. Add to that, the real or imagined belief that employment of equal status and reward would not be forthcoming, and especially late career employees feel trapped. The trend does appear to carry over in the other two reactions as well, but definitely not as strongly: uncertain managers tend to be in early to middle career, and contrary managers tend to be mid-career.

ORGANIZATIONAL RESPONSES TO MIDDLE MANAGERS

In examining our data for organizational responses intended to help middle managers cope with change, we were struck with the limited variety of responses. Predominantly, executives and senior managers from our sites seemed to be unaware of middle managers' negative reactions as a problem which they, as initiators and leaders of changes, needed to address directly. We were able to identify seven types of activities which executives and senior managers undertook as responses to middle managers:

1 Expecting middle managers to get on with their work without any particular assistance or response, while more changes of the kind causing the reaction continue, is probably the most common organizational response.
2 Offering education and training courses stands out as one of the most frequent responses.
3 Carrying out an attitude survey of some kind is another typical response.
4 Senior managers introduce team briefing and company newsletters as a response to complaints about lack of communications.

5 Often as a part of legal changes related to business strategy, executives will alter the bonus or incentive systems of middle managers, in particular, or employees, more generally.

6 Stating explicitly or implicitly that 'those who don't like the changes can leave' appears in our data as a more common response to negative middle managers than would be publicly admitted.

7 In two of the action research projects, executives and senior managers have experimented with forums for working through negative reactions with their middle managers.

DISCUSSION

We have presented an argument for understanding middle managers' negative reactions to organizational change. Executives, senior managers, organizational development consultants, and operational personnel often complain about resistance to change coming precisely from middle managers. 'They just can't let go of power' is a favourite explanation of their resistance. Hopefully, we have offered a more comprehensive rationale for why middle managers might not embrace organizational changes.

A basic conclusion of work presented in this chapter is that middle managers are being subjected to multiple changes in what is expected of them in terms of knowledge, motivation, goals and means, role behaviours and ethics. Further, that these changes take place without acknowledgement of their psychological impact on middle managers.

We developed a crude typology of three degrees of negative reaction: uncertainty, contrariness and the double-bind. Evidence for these reactions were readily apparent from our data. A more detailed analysis of scenarios, written to describe middle managers from seven of our sites, resulted in some descriptive differences between these three groups of middle managers who react negatively. A second conclusion of the material presented in this chapter, therefore, is that middle managers are impacted psychologically to different degrees depending on the stage of their career and on the availability of viable options offered by their employing organization.

In terms of future research in this area, first we need to know more about the relationship between middle managers' expectations, commitment and performance, and the impact of organizational responses on middle managers' reactions. Second, we need to know more about how expectations can be adjusted if one realizes that they are apparently too high – or too low, for that matter. Third, the multi-dimensionality of the contract and how it changes over time needs further study. The middle manager job is very suitable for such an analysis due to the turbulence of the job environment of this particular occupational group. Finally, our exploratory study does not support the idea that the more contractual elements implicated in an organizational change, the stronger the emotional reaction. All three degrees of reactions show a range of between two and four elements affected. A more detailed study, with a better method of judging elements, would need to be developed. That said, there did seem to be particular trends in which aspects of the changes bothered middle managers most. The uncertain managers most often mentioned career prospects; the contrary managers complained of increased responsibility simultaneously with decreased resources and power; and double-bind managers spoke of loss of status and power. These trends suggest that a clearer conceptual framework, linking contractual elements to organizational practices, might be able to pick up commonalities among middle managers with different emotional reactions.

REFERENCES

Argyris, C. (1964) *Integrating the Individual and the Organisation*, New York: J. Wiley.

Bateson, G. (1972) *Steps to an Ecology of Mind: A Revolutionary Approach to Man's Understanding of Himself*, New York: Ballantine Books.

Dopson, S. and Neumann, J.E. (1994) 'Uncertainty, contrariness and the double-bind: middle managers' reactions to their changing contracts', Templeton College Research Paper.

Gowler, D. (1978) 'Job satisfaction: values and contracts', in K. Legge and E. Mumford (eds) *Designing Organizations for Satisfaction and Efficiency*, Farnborough: Gower, 36–55.

Kotter, J.P. (1982) 'The psychological contract: managing the joining up process', *California Management Review* 15, Spring: 91–9.

Louis M.R. (1980) 'Surprise and sense making: what newcomer's experience in entering unfamiliar organizational settings', *Administrative Science Quarterly*, 25: 226.

Mumford, E. (1978) 'Job satisfaction: a method of analysis', in K. Legge and E.N. Mumford (eds) *Designing Organizations for Satisfaction and Efficiency*, Farnborough: Gower, 18–33.

Neumann, J.E. (1989) 'Why people don't participate in organizational change', in R.W. Woodman and W.A. Pasmore (eds) *Research in Organizational Change and Development*, **3**, Greenwich, CT: JAI Press, 181–212.

Newell, H. and Dopson, S. (1994) 'Middle management careers', a case study of BT, Warwick University Industrial Relations Unit Research Paper.

Nicholson, N. and Johns, G. (1985) 'The absence culture and the psychological contract – who is in control of absence?', *Academy of Management Review* **10**(3): 397–407.

Rousseau, D.M. (1990) 'New higher perceptions of their own and their employers' obligations: a study of psychological contracts'. *The Journal of Organizational Behaviour* **11**: 389–400.

Schein, E.H. (1980) 'Organizational socialization and the profession of management', in D. Kolb, I.R. Rubin and J.M. McIntyre (eds) *Organizational Psychology: A Book of Readings*, 3rd edn, Englewood Cliffs, NJ: Prentice Hall, 9–23.

— (1985) *Organizational Psychology*, 3rd edn, Englewood Cliffs NJ: Prentice Hall.

Thierry, H. (1984) 'Motivation and satisfaction', in H. Thierry, P.J. Drenth, P.J. Willems and C.J. de Wolff (eds) *Handbook of Work and Organizational Psychology*, **1**, Chichester: John Wiley, 131–74.

Wanous, J.P. (1980) *Organizational Entry: Recruitment, Selection and Socialization of Newcomers*, Reading, MA: Addison-Wesley.

11

EUROPEAN PROFESSIONAL AND MANAGERIAL STAFF ON THE MOVE

Michel Rousselot

Questions relating to the role, the definition, the future of professional and managerial staff[1] (P&MS) are frequently asked by
employers or trade unionists, by sociologists or management
theorists; to the extent that even if the content changes this
constant questioning tends to prove that middle managers
(P&MS) do in fact have an important role to play in companies
and in society. Unlike the previous chapters which were based
on academic observations, I will outline the position of P&MS
based on experience and consultations with professionals and
managers in various countries. In the pursuit of international
competition, it is well known that P&MS form intricate groups,
as well as being innovators, initiators, necessary go-betweens in
organizations and social models.

SOCIO-PROFESSIONAL DIVERSITY AND IDENTITY

The diversity and heterogeneity of professional identities,
together with the changes of the past decades have impacted
upon P&MS, whether they are skilled professionals or managers
working in small private firms, in large manufacturing groups
or in the public sector. The plurality of cultures and national
systems of training have led not only to diverse forms of work
organization, but also to different methods of social representation and organization. However, because of the existence of
similar professional responsibilities, the French expression
'cadres', sometimes regarded as impossible to translate and
specific to a national situation, does express the same profes-

sional realities as English 'professional and managerial staff', German 'Fach und Fürhungskräfte' and is similar to Italian 'quadri', Spanish 'cuadros', Portuguese 'quadros' and Flemish or German Swiss 'kader' (see Chapter 2).

The debate over the precise limits of the professional and managerial staff's group may, as in any border dispute, create such complex misunderstandings that, depending on the countries, could affect salaries, social rights, status. The increase in qualifications, the evolution of managerial methods and the similarities in ways of life tend to erase the differences between P&MS and the most skilled technicians or other associate professionals. Some past barriers are fading away; however, due to rising unemployment and economic competition, access to managerial positions is not getting any easier. The identity of a changing socio-professional group cannot be defined by its limits but by its contents.

Therefore, some elements still constitute common identifying references and common typical behaviours for P&MS. Two elements are especially significant: a higher level of education and skills acquired through basic or continuous training or through experience and, the practice of some professional responsibilities that lead to a broader vision. It was agreed at international level to use these two elements as basic references for the first international definition of P&MS formulated during a tripartite conference (workers, employers, governments) by the International Labour Organization (ILO) in 1977 (see Chapter 2) and has since been included in the international standard classification of occupations, ISCO-88.[2] Its use by the European Union statistic services, EUROSTAT will make it possible to present coherent information about jobs and occupations between countries in the future.

PRESENT UNCERTAINTY

Professional and management staff were prime movers in the first three decades after the Second World War. Their numbers increased considerably (often tripled) and the technical progress they represented, encouraged economic development. The period which followed has been quite different. The world economy has moved towards deregulation and growing competition, creating, particularly in Europe, economic difficulties and massive unemployment to the point of social exclusion for the most deprived.

Over the years, the number of P&MS has increased largely in the service sector and their role has fundamentally changed. Activities for leading and regulating have often taken over from technical activities. Consequently, highly skilled professionals often find it difficult to have their abilities recognized unless they possess associated managerial functions. Moreover, modern management methods have developed under various and fashionable terminologies. They frequently lead to flat organizations with a reduced number of middle-level positions and team work with more autonomy and initiative but under computerized central controls. Management of human and social dimensions has taken a more important place with staff participation models, which has resulted in new competition between management and unions. For P&MS, complexity, that Taylorism attempted to reduce, has become prevalent again with the management of unexpected factors and the differing rationalities of numerous interlocutors.

Professional and managerial staff have never stopped investing in their professional activity. Fast evolution makes it absolutely necessary not only to update one's knowledge and abilities but also to adapt the training content. No diploma, however prestigious, can guarantee a lifelong career. Continuous training has been playing an increasing role for P&MS, as they themselves are training other workers. Even though measures to evaluate abilities or systems to recognize professional experience are developing, they are still too limited in number.

Innovators, educators, trainers, crisis managers, P&MS in all European countries consider motivation and responsibility as the most important element in the firm. The Conseils-Sondages-Analyses (CSA) study 'P&MS in Europe 1994'[3] has confirmed that this choice is persistent even though relations with companies have fundamentally changed.

A number of tensions have, indeed, been developing in European companies as well as in public services and administration over the last decade. Performance-related pay systems have too often been individualized secretly without negotiation, reducing the credibility of the proceedings. Moreover, financial and trading imperatives at numerous levels have been added to the speed of technological and organizational change, and constraints caused by some management methods (such as 'lean production') and information technologies. Those who have preserved their jobs often work harder and harder. Some activities have been suppressed or contracted out. Some P&MS had no choice other than to take an independent and precarious consultant position. P&MS unemployment, which for a long time remained lower than unemployment in other groups, has grown suddenly and quickly in the last three years in all European countries.[4] Young graduates have been severely affected. Overwork or unemployment have often become two aspects of the same reality. It is easy to understand why P&MS's trust in companies might thus be threatened or broken.

Moreover, managerial methods supposedly based on participation have often shown that strategic choices were still the prerogative of a generally very limited number of top managers and were the result of secret decisions. During periods of reorganization with important effects on companies' and workers' futures, P&MS and top managers have moved apart from one another, especially in large companies.

We must add that, in Central and Eastern Europe, restoring democracy and a new market economy has created new groups of managers and has had important effects on P&MS's functions.[5]

STAKES FOR THE FUTURE

Globalization of economies, directly or indirectly touches all economic practices. Technologies are world-wide even if markets remain sectoral in some cases. Partnerships, reorganizations, strategies are growing in a world-wide field. But at the end of the twentieth century, the lack of sufficient world-wide regulation generates financial confusion, unbalanced development, social stresses, misery, famines and wars. World-wide organizations such as United Nations Organization (UNO), ILO or the new World Trade Organization (WTO) are slowly trying to take up the challenge. The states who were exerting, the main regulating functions in separated economies some decades ago, no longer have the necessary instruments, and thus the problems are beyond the limits of their competence. Between the tardiness of world-wide institutions and the poor adaptation of the states, isn't there any other option? Areas of economic integration have appeared in Asia, North America and South America. The European Union, carried by political will, is trying to harmonize economic and social union. Is not the regional/continental level, therefore, the correct base upon which to build and where the resources to implement the necessary decisions are located? Here is one possible solution to the problem of economic and social development. In Europe, we have institutions, policies, and instruments we can seize. So, for European P&MS opportunities appear which we will summarize under the next four headings.

Strengthening the European Union

According to the CSA poll, mentioned above,[6] between 82 per cent and 95 per cent of P&MS are strongly in favour of the principle of European construction and of strengthening the European Union itself. This is not an idealized vision as they are very much aware of the inherent difficulties and obstacles. Therefore we are somewhat obliged to successfully reform the treaties and institutions (forecast for 1996), to master large-scale and structural unemployment, and to realize a single currency. This also requires a better economic coherence supported by efficient public services, by infrastructure investments (especially for large trans-European networks and information highways) and by industrial policies promoting the development of an economic network of competing firms, under world-wide competition, but with European decision centres.

Opening up to Central and Eastern European countries and restoring the balance of exchanges with developing countries constitute challenges that the European Union must take up with its economic weight and its political will.

Promoting a model of European management

Management systems are not independent from social patterns. European firms have been confronted with a succession of trends, mostly from America and Japan. They have borrowed here and there. However, European dynamism is accelerating the emergence of a European pattern of management. As two German managers observe in the study 'Euromanagement':[7] 'if one considers only Europe, there are differences between the countries in the way they manage a company, but viewed globally from the outside the differences between Europe, the United States and Japan make Europe appear homogeneous'.

Facing American management marked by individualism, competition, professionalism, immediate profit – and Japanese management – based on social integration, consensus, long-term, quality – European vision is characterized by adaptation to international diversity, respect for individuals, internal negotiation and collective bargaining, social responsibility of the firms based on important social protection devices, recognition of union rights even for P&MS.[8] Simultaneously it implies taking account of the economic and social dimension of their reciprocal actions. It looks for ways and means, in various forms according to countries and social cultures to create industrial democracy which sometimes includes consultation systems related to strategic choices which have just been recognized at European level by the recent directive concerning European works councils.

Professional and managerial staff are playing a major part in this European management model emergence which is gradually changing their activities and responsibilities: administrative (relations with salaried employees and trade unions) as well as functional (intervention into management and work organization practices).

Securing freedom of movement in Europe

Free movement of goods, capital or services and mobility of persons will go hand in hand. Professional and management staff are especially concerned. In order to be humane, mobility must first be recognized as a freedom and not an obligation. Moreover, many problems must be resolved, such as those concerning taxes, social protection (especially supplementary pension), partner's employment, children's scholarship and career, especially on returning to the country of origin (see Table 11.1).

Thus it is indispensable to develop joint devices in Europe, allowing us to improve information on P&MS European labour market (as EURES – European Employment Service), to harmonize tax rules, to link social protection and pension systems and also to create precise guarantees through European legislation and through European collective negotiation at a central or

Table 11.1 Obstacles to working in another European country

	5 countries, combined result %	France %	Germany %	United Kingdom %	Italy %	Spain %
Language barriers	46	42	44	55	40	50
Fear of not finding another job if one job did not work out	33	40	34	44	22	25
Uncertainty about children's education	25	27	30	40	13	17
Lack of knowledge of the job market	25	25	27	27	19	26
Uncertainty about social security benefits	24	30	48	19	14	8
Inadequate recognition of qualifications and diplomas	23	21	39	18	16	21
Uncertainty about retirement benefits	22	22	43	27	12	8
Uncertainty about partner's employment	21	24	24	28	16	14
Lack of knowledge of employment contracts and collective agreements	20	21	26	26	12	16
Inadequate tax harmonization	9	9	14	14	3	5

Note: Percentages represent the views of people interviewed in each country.

Source: Survey 'P&MS in Europe 1994' conducted by CSA institute (Paris) in October 1994 among P&MS in five European countries, for UCC (Engineers' and Managers' Union (FDT) with the European Commission support.

sectorial level and at the multinational groups' level too. EURO-CADRES formulated propositions in these fields, and the European Union's social action programme (published in April 1995) has retained several initiatives whose adoption and implementation it is hoped will not be delayed.

Recognizing qualifications and diplomas

European recognition of qualifications is progressing too slowly. Salaried employees at every level are concerned. However, work undertaken for labour qualifications was stopped and vital decisions taken for regulated professions, especially concerning the right to practise which do not grant recognition of qualifications certified by a diploma nor those acquired through professional experience. A device was created for engineers but it has no juridical effect since it has a private origin.[9]

EUROCADRES insisted, and succeeded in reopening discussion on recognition of higher level qualifications and diplomas. It led to a European Commission's communication which, in spring 1995, was discussed with EUROCADRES P&MS's organizations in various countries. Significant progress in this field would be useful to firms and would allow the evolution of training systems. Winning clear and coherent recognition systems is a challenge for European P&MS. It is one of the mobility keys and ought to be a constitutive element of European citizenship.

PROFESSIONAL AND MANAGERIAL STAFF ON THE MOVE

Confronted with changes and uncertainties touching all fields of their practices and responsibilities, facing challenges which they discern, but the scale of which often surpasses individual abilities, many European P&MS did not remain passive. They gathered in associations, in trade unions of various forms according to countries. This movement is unified in the Council of European P&MS, EUROCADRES,[10] recognized as a European social partner and working jointly with the European Trade Unions Confederation, ETUC. Today the majority of P&MS are in favour of the development of a European trade-unionism (see Table 11.2).

For P&MS, it is therefore becoming possible at European level to have instruments of exchange, information and intervention. For P&MS, European construction is not simply a global and remote political creation, but constitutes combined professional interests. It concerns their professional practices by recognizing abilities and diplomas, mobility, management conception and their implication in economic and social decisions.

Table 11.2 Degree of opinion favourable towards the development of a European trade-unionism

	5 countries, combined result %	France %	Germany %	United Kingdom %	Italy %	Spain %
Yes	56	51	53	42	75	58
No	44	49	47	58	25	42

Note: Percentages represent the views of people interviewed in each country.

Source: Survey 'P&MS in Europe 1994' conducted by CSA institute (Paris) in October 1994 among P&MS in five European countries, for UCC (Engineers' and Managers' Union CFDT) with the European Commission support.

NOTES

1 In this article we shall use the expression 'professional and managerial staff' (P&MS) as having the same meaning as 'middle managers'. As a matter of fact, 'middle managers' do not always have managerial functions when many 'professionals' have. Their levels of abilities and responsibilities are higher than those of 'technicians' or 'supervisors'.

2 ISCO established in 1988 (unlike the previous from 1968) classifies 'legislators, senior officials and managers' in the first group and 'professionals' in the second group. A third group concerns 'technicians and associate professionals'

3 See 'P&MS in Europe 1994' survey conducted by CSA (institute of analysis, poll and advices) among P&MS in five European countries, for UCC (Engineers' and Managers' union CFDT) with the European Commission support.

4 See EUROCADRES studies and also the booklet 'European P&MS for employment' a report of the symposium held in Brussels in September 1994.

5 Intervention of Professor Mihaly Csako from sociology institute of Eotvos Lorand University, Budapest, during FIET seminar held in Budapest in June 1992.

6 See 'P&MS in Europe 1994' survey conducted by CSA institute among P&MS in five European countries, for UCC (Engineers' and Managers' union CFDT) with the European Commission support.

7 See 'Euromanagement' published by Kogan Page (London) and 'L'art du management européen' published by Editions d'Organisation (Paris), a study made at the request of the European industrialists' Round Table by H. Bloom, R. Calori and P. de Woot with ESC Lyon Group.

8 P&MS's union rights are still coming up against practical but also juridical obstacles in many countries. In spite of ILO instructions,

it's especially the case in the United States and in several Asian countries for P&MS with authority over other persons. See 'P&MS: their place in the labour relations system of Canada and the United States' by M. Bendel and 'Les droits syndicaux des cadres: une perspective internationale' by C. Dupont-Sakharov and L. Frexinos, sectoral activities programme working papers, ILO (Geneva), and the ILO 'Compendium of principles and good practices relating to the employment of professional workers', (Geneva).

9 'EUR-ING' system was created by FEANI (European Federation of Engineers National Associations).

10 As a general estimate, some 10 to 15 per cent of employed persons hold professional and/or managerial posts. EUROCADRES, the Council of European Professional and Managerial Staff groups more than four million members in Western Europe according to ISCO 88 (2) groups 1 and 2, in all branches of industry, private companies, public services and administrative departments. It is the main organization of P&MS in Europe. EUROCADRES has established contacts with the various European institutions and organizations at all levels, and is recognized as a European social partner. The Council conducts surveys and studies, organizes exchanges of information and runs conferences. It puts forward proposals and intervenes in all issues involving P&MS.

12

CONCLUSIONS

Yves-Frédéric Livian and John G. Burgoyne

Middle management is a subject generating a .discourse of remarkable stability. Middle managers (MMs) are still recognized as the key to company performance, and at the same time are often viewed as 'reluctant to change'. They carry a large part of an organization's experience and executives are seeking to renew their competence, through injection of 'new blood' and education or training. They are a stable element of organizations, but also always in search of their identity. Many people speak for them, but they do not very often speak themselves.

Today, the question is again posed: what are the roles, if any, of MMs in emergent forms of organization, adapted to highly competitive and moving environments? Are we living a period of complete transformation (from which will result a new configuration of this group) or a period of incremental adaptations, of convergence or divergence?

We have tried in this book to provide some answers to these questions on the basis of one of the first European overviews on this subject. We now synthetize and extend the reflections that these contributions can induce. Before doing so, we would like to emphasize that our conclusions are drawn in a specific perspective, which consists in approaching the MM reality from an organizational view. We have seen that there are several ways of distinguishing a group like MMs, we have chosen the organization one, but we know that if we adopt other points of view, the analysis of the MM group raises questions which have not been addressed in this book. We have seen that the categorization of intermediate social groups is primarily a matter of contingent construction in a specific societal context, and that there are very different realities in that respect throughout Europe.

There is another crucial aspect which is not dealt with in our book, which is the MM level of education and their position in a social path. In that respect too, we certainly would have seen various realities, according to the institutional context and the structure of élite formation process existing in each country.

In the same perspective, our methodology did not allow us to take into account as deeply as necessary, the national cultural variables affecting the position and roles of MM. However, we have seen examples where managerial models, using cultural norms, strongly influence organizational situations: greater centralization in French public companies, based on a culturally rooted conception of leadership; importance of managerial legitimacy in the British and Dutch contexts in the private sector; strong decentralization in the Danish context; centralization and procedural controls in Greek public services. We could also assume (but we have very few elements about this in our studies) that the ways MMs adapt or react to these situations are affected by national (but also professional) cultures.

Two general conclusions can be drawn.

THE RATE OF CHANGE MAY BE SLOWER THAN FREQUENTLY ASSUMED

The material provided in this book gives a balanced view of the importance of changes experienced in Europe. A number of studies show little 'objective' change in MM roles, positions and conditions of employment. In the five-countries study, but also in other analysis based on local realities (France, Greece), the rate of change is less quick than was expected. Other chapters have emphasized changes, mainly in communication and HR roles. Is there a contradiction between these two kinds of results? Even if we cannot reject the hypothesis of contradictory results (because of the large diversity of the realities observed and the different methodologies used in this book), we feel that these differences mainly are the result of difference of perspectives.

We can draw a clear conclusion from our material about the kind of change in organizational forms that is experienced: except in some large and innovative companies trying to experience new models of management the rate of change is rather slow. Change is slow in the public bureaucracies, either because of very limited efforts of change, or because of its newness and intrinsic difficulty. It is also slower than assumed in the private sector, where a number of companies are attempting to function more flexibly, but cannot avoid developing control process or increasing the weight of formal procedures. Change is slow also because of the weight of leader-focused styles in small-sized companies, which does not allow enough autonomy to the intermediate levels, when they exist.

This does not mean that MMs are in a stable situation and are not feeling changes, at least partly, about what is expected from them and about their 'psychological contracts' linking them to their employers. The feeling of pressure on performance and lateral co-operation, and of increased commitment to business operations, can be found even if there is not a complete transformation of their roles and of the structures in which they operate.

One dimension which can contribute to explain these results is the evolution of MM characteristics. Confronted with the same organizational contexts, new populations are adopting different strategies. In our book, reference is made to the expectations of better educated MMs, who are sometimes disappointed by the low rate of organizational change (for example, in France). We have seen also the different reactions of managers due to their position in the career curve (in France and the UK). In the meantime, older or more traditional populations fear organizational changes and are expecting the maintenance of the system which they have been used to. Reactions and attitudes towards a certain rate of change vary according to the personal resources that individuals hold.

THERE IS A STRONG CONVERGENCE IN THE MIDDLE MANAGER'S ORGANIZATIONAL SITUATION

There are sector and national differences on many subjects. In the private sector, we have seen that few companies have reduced the number of layers or transformed the MM position in the organizational process (such a change was found only in one of the British and Dutch cases, and in Denmark) while most organizations observed have not experienced such a move. There are differences in the style of management and the type of hierarchical relations between large advanced companies and traditional small-sized ones. In some cases, MMs are already endowed with a wide autonomy and responsibilty over people. In other cases (more frequent in our view) they are strongly linked with organizational procedures and have few possibilities of impacting the management of human resources.

In the public sector, there is a clearly contrasting picture between two types of situations. On one hand, very traditional bureaucracies seem to expect from their managers routinized tasks, linked with the enforcement of official rules (for example, Greece). On the other, recent efforts of modernization take the form of the development of new practices: decentralization, performance appraisal, communication. But this evolution takes place in the context of a managerial discourse which is not always adapted to the realities as viewed by middle managers themselves (for example, France). In spite of these differences, the convergence is remarkable. This convergence is not due to a common so-called 'Euromanager' profile, but more in our opinion to the similarity of the major trends affecting the economic environnement in the countries observed.

Middle managers are working hard on translating, adapting, implementing and controlling strategic orientations which they have rarely contributed to. They are oriented towards obtaining, through the people and the equipment at their disposal, concrete business results on which they are strongly controlled and against which they are evaluated. They are helping to implement and enforce new quality requirements. Middle managers are expected to develop a wide range of the same behavioural skills, in order to smooth operational relations and manage unavoidable conflicts. They have to constantly build their legitimacy, somewhere between technical know-how and managerial talent.

Another general observation is the lack of support, or only weak support, received from the upper levels of the organization and the scarcity of the programmes devoted to their development. There are some answers to this problem in training terms, but they appear to be very limited.

Therefore, it is understandable that similar conditions seem to induce similar reactions and attitudes, at the same career stage. Several analyses, in different countries and sectors, show MM discomfort at mid-career, often due to the difficulty of remaining effective under the now stronger and more complex pressure. This discomfort is increased by a strong feeling of lack of recognition and lack of a clear view of their own development.

We propose that the following items need to be addressed:

1 In most of the situations observed MMs are lacking social and symbolic recognition. They are members of an 'intermediate' group which is not easily readable. Their role is crucial, top managers say, but very few MMs seem to be socially rewarded. Many are experiencing a very strenuous situation, subordinate to operational and strategic decisions mostly taken at a higher level.

2 Middle manager's views of organizational expectations often seem ambiguous. Many MMs seem caught between managerial rhetorics (decentralization, autonomy, entrepreneurship behaviour) and day-to-day constraints (getting results, in the market sector, or enforcing the rules, in public administrations). They could expect more clarity in the message conceived by the upper levels. Training and supporting programmes, specially tailored to their needs, and taking into account their particular situation, seem to be very rare. Effective career orientation and management is also lacking, confirming many observations about the concentration of career development policies on high-level managers and executives, or only on those in the MM range considered as 'high potentials'.

3 This does not mean that MMs are passive. Our study gives scattered but positive insights on MMs willing to adapt to change, conceiving a personal project of development, attending formal training for further strenghthening of their competence. But it appears that this could be greatly supported by organization policies genuinely wishing to develop their performance through middle management effectiveness.

Without that effort, MMs' problems will remain only an element of senior executives' rhetoric.

INDEX

209

trade unionists 194
training courses *see* education
    and training courses

unbalanced development 197
uncertainty 174, 191
unemployment 196
unity of command 96

visible commitment 182; *see also*
    commitment
Vorstandmitglieder 30

wars 197

zero defects 157